Russell Earls Davis graduated in Law at Sydney University and practised as a solicitor in Sydney for a short time before attending Theological College and entering the ministry of the Anglican Church. Invited to become Precentor of Saint George's Cathedral in Perth, he moved to Western Australia.

When Hale School – Perth's oldest school for boys – became a Church School in 1960, he was appointed as its Chaplain. During 28 years as Chaplain at Hale School he taught History, was the Master in Charge of the Junior School for seven years and played a part in the development of Rugby Union in Western Australia, in the Public Schools Association and at Hale in particular.

After retiring, he took up the challenge of qualifying for the legal profession in Western Australia, was admitted as a solicitor and practised for seven years before retiring again and occupying his spare time by writing.

In 2010 his account of the role of William Bligh as the fourth governor of New South Wales was published by Woodslane under the title *Bligh in Australia*. He then set out to write an account of the events that resulted in Western Australia becoming the economic powerhouse of Australia. The result of over a year of research and writing is *A Concise History of Western Australia*.

WESTERN AUSTRALIA

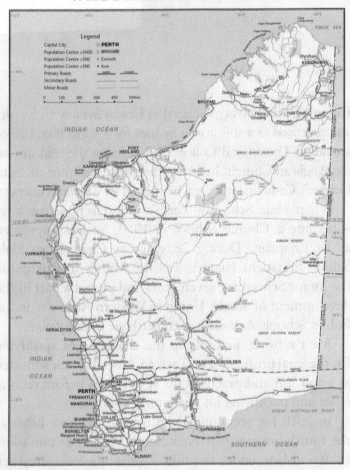

Western Australia map above courtesy of Landgate.

The cover image Map of Western Australia and magnifying glass is courtesy of iStock

The seperator icon of the man and lady used through out this book, and first used on page 42, has been taken from the picture *South View of Sydney* painted by V. Woodhouse, c. 1802 - courtesy of National Library of Australia.

WESTERN AUSTRALIA

RUSSELL EARLS DAVIS

Woodslane Press Pty Ltd
7/5 Vuko Place, Warriewood, NSW 2102
Email: info@woodslane.com.au
Website: www.woodslane.com.au

First published in Australia in 2012 by Woodslane Press
© 2012 Woodslane Press, text © 2012 Russell Earls Davis

National Library of Australia Cataloguing-in-Publication entry

Author:	Davis, Russell Earls.
Title:	A concise history of Western Australia / Russell Earls Davis.
ISBN:	9781921874642 (pbk.)
Notes:	Includes bibliographical references and index.
Subjects:	Western Australia--History
Dewey Number:	994.1

Design and layout by Jenny Cowan
Printed in Australia by SOS Print + Media

Contents

Introduction

So much has happened in the lives of the millions of people who have lived in Western Australia that all the libraries of the world would not be enough to house the books that would have to be written to record every detail.

All any historian can do is chronicle those facts he or she considers to be important or of special interest, and that usually means that the historian's prejudices and values influence what is written.

With regard to values, I believe it is not fair to judge the actions of past generations by standards that are commonly accepted in modern times. In writing this concise history I have endeavoured to be non-judgemental and to record what happened without praise or condemnation. As a result, this record of Western Australian history will probably not please everyone.

In selecting what to include I have simply chosen incidents and facts that seemed to me to be particularly interesting or to have had long-term consequences for Western Australia.

Chapter 1: *The First Immigrants*

When humans first arrived in Australia is a matter of debate among anthropologists. At one stage it was widely accepted that all humankind descended from *Homo sapiens* that evolved in Africa and then spread throughout the World. How primitive humans managed to cross the seas was explained by theorizing that an ice age provided ice bridges and reduced sea levels or, alternatively, that movements of tectonic plates caused the raising of land bridges that have subsequently disappeared.

The 1974 discovery of the complete skeleton of a man buried near Mungo Lake in western New South Wales cast some doubt on the 'Out of Africa' theory. The skeleton was estimated to be 40,000 years old and, while it is like the skeleton of a modern Australian aboriginal, its DNA is different from that of modern aborigines and Europeans. If the 'Out of Africa' theory is correct, all mankind should have similar mitochondrial DNA. Some anthropologists have explained Mungo Man's odd DNA by advocating a theory of Multiregional Evolution. They claim that a variety of human beings, unrelated to those who came out of Africa, must have evolved and lived in Australia before becoming extinct.

Wherever the truth lies, humans of some sort (or sorts) have lived in Australia for a long time – more than 40,000 years or as much as 125,000 years according to some anthropologists.

Early Australians multiplied and spread until they could be found in almost every part of the country. Those who migrated to the west of the island-continent found life far more difficult than did those who chose to live in the east. The eastern seaboard has rivers that flow all year round and vast areas with vegetation that can support a variety of animal life. In comparison, a large part of Western Australia is desert so dry that life of any sort is faced with a struggle to survive. Three deserts – the Great Sandy Desert, the Gibson Desert and the Great Victoria Desert – and the Nullarbor Plain cover more than half of the state.

Some Australian aboriginals did manage to adapt to living in the hot, dry areas of Western Australia by hunting and gathering in small family groups, ranging over wide areas in the search for food, and learning where to find sources of water. Out of necessity, the number of these groups always remained small. The great majority of the Indigenous Australians in the west chose to hunt and gather in the areas with a higher rainfall – the tropical north and the far south-west.

The indigenous Australians were still hunters and gatherers when the Europeans arrived. That they did not become nomadic herdsmen – one step taken by humans towards civilisation in other lands – could perhaps be explained by the fact that Australia's native animals are not suitable for domestication. That they had never settled down to become farmers could be explained by the fact that Australia did not have the grasses such as wheat and rice that were vital in the development of agriculture in other lands. Agriculture allowed people to form settled communities and cultivate the social structures, skills and technologies of civilisation. 'Civilisation' is here used in its basic meaning, being – the characteristics of an urbanised society.

Without domesticated animals – other than the dingoes – or plants suitable for cropping, Australian aboriginals survived by roaming the countryside, hunting animals for meat and gathering the fruits of the natural vegetation. The only cultivation of the land that they attempted was the clearing of patches of vegetation, using fire, in order to create larger areas of grazing for animals, which made the hunting easier. In some ways it is almost understandable that the explorers landing in Australia considered the land to be *terra nullius* – land owned by no one – as there were none of the indications of land ownership they had known in Europe.

In 1688 William Dampier, a privateer, sailed into King Sound in the north of Western Australia and wrote the first description in English of the land and the Australian aboriginals living there.

New Holland is a very large tract of land. It is not yet determined if it is an island or a main continent, but I am certain it joins neither Asia, Africa nor America.This part of it that we saw is all low even land ... of a dry sandy soil, destitute of water except you make wells, yet producing diverse sorts of trees but the woods are not thick nor the trees very big.

Regarding the indigenous Australians, Dampier wrote:

The inhabitants of this country are the miser-ablest people in the world. The Hodmadods of Monomotapa though a nasty people, yet for wealth are gentlemen to these, who have no houses and no skin garments, sheep, poultry and fruits of the earth, ostrich eggs, etc as the Hodmadods have.And, setting aside their human shape, they differ but little from brutes. They are tall, straight-bodied and thin with small, long limbs. They have great heads, round foreheads and great brows. Their eyelids are always half closed to keep out the flies; they being so troublesome here that no fanning will keep them from coming to one's face and without the assistance of both hands to keep them off they will creep into one's nostrils and mouth too if the lips are not shut very close.[1]

Over the millennia, the indigenous peoples of Western Australia developed regional languages and physical characteristics. There came to be four main groups: the tribes or clans in the Kimberley, the Noongar in the south, the Yamatji in the central districts and the Wangai in what is now known as the Goldfields.

---

1   J Masefield (ed), Dampier's Voyages, vol 1, E.Grant Richards, London, 1906, p437 et seq.

Chapter 2: *Arrival Of The Europeans*

The expansion of European societies in the fifteenth and sixteenth centuries saw a dramatic increase in trade and importation from the Far East. Asia was a rich source of the exotic goods that were in high demand among the Europeans. Conveying goods from the Far East to Europe over land was slow, hazardous and inefficient. It was sailors from Portugal who pioneered a sea route to India, and the Dutch soon followed them. Most important to the history of Australia were the Dutch trading posts in what was called the Spice Islands – now known as Indonesia. From the Spice Islands Dutch sailors set out to explore adjacent lands.

In 1606, Willem Jansz sailed his ship, the *Duyfken* into the Gulf of Carpentaria and went ashore at Cape York. His report discouraged any further exploration of the vast island–continent that cartographers had named New Holland. When Abel Tasman set off on a journey of exploration in 1644, he had instructions not to waste time looking at New Holland because the *Duyfken* expedition 'only ascertained that vast regions were for the greater part uncultivated, and certain parts inhabited by savage, cruel, black barbarians who slew some of our sailors.'[2] Tasman sailed well south of mainland Australia and discovered Tasmania and New Zealand.

In 1623, men from another Dutch ship under the command of Jan Carstenz went ashore at Cape York. Carstenz reported:

> It is very dry and barren for, during all the time we have searched and examined this part of the coast to our best ability, we have not seen one fruit-bearing tree nor anything that man make use of; there are no mountains or hills, so it may be safely concluded that the land contains no metals, nor yields any precious woods such as sandalwood, aloes or Columba. In our judgement this is the most arid and barren region that could be found anywhere on the earth. The inhabitants, too, are the most wretched that I have ever seen..."[3]

Not surprisingly the Dutch, in view of such reports as those, never did bother to set up trading posts in Australia. Their ships did occasionally visit the coast of Western Australia, often than not without intending to do so. These unintended visits were due to the risky route they followed to the Spice Islands.

At first the European sailors rounded the southernmost point of Africa, sailed north along the eastern coast, and then cut across the Indian Ocean. In 1611, Hendrik Brouwer pioneered a new route to the Spice Islands.

2 JE Heeres (ed.), *Abel Janszoon Tasman's Journal of his Discovery of Van Diemen's land and New Zealand, Kovach,* Los Angeles, 1965, p38.
3 JE Heeres (ed.), *The Part Borne by the Dutch in the Discovery of Australia 1606-1765,* Luzac & Co London , 1899, p39.

He sailed south from the Cape of Good Hope until he reached the latitude where there is a constant westerly wind – the Roaring Forties. With the strong wind behind him, he sailed rapidly eastward until he calculated he had reached the longitude of the Spice Islands, turned northwards and reached Batavia many weeks before he would have had he followed the established route across the Indian Ocean. Soon all Dutch captains were following Brouwer's course. However, gauging when to turn northwards along Brouwer's route became a serious problem because navigators had no way to estimate longitude accurately. It was not until the latter half of the eighteenth century that marine chronometers were sufficiently refined to allow longitude to be determined with reasonable certitude. As a result of longitude miscalculations some ships went too far eastwards and were wrecked on the coast of Western Australia.

In 1622, the *Trial,* owned by the British East India Company, set off for Batavia carrying a large amount of silver to be used for trade. It went too far eastwards and was wrecked when it struck a submerged rock near Barrow Island. Ninety three men drowned as their ship went down, but the captain – John Brooke – his son and nine others managed to leave the wreck in a skiff. Thirty five other seamen were able to board a longboat and together the two small boats sailed to Batavia with the loss of just one life. Brooke and his crew would have been the first Britons to come to Western Australia.

In October 1628, a convoy of eight ships set out from Holland to sail to the Spice Islands. In command of a ship

named the *Batavia* on its maiden voyage was Francesco
Pelsaert. The convoy became scattered and, some sixty
kilometres off the coast of Western Australia, the *Batavia*
ran aground at the Abrolhos Islands. The passengers – a
few women and a small detachment of French soldiers –
were set ashore on one island with a few members of the
crew while the rest were landed on a nearby island. There
they remained for over four months while Pelsaert and
some of the sailors used small lifeboats to sail to Batavia
for help. Those he left behind on the islands could claim
the distinction of being the first Europeans to settle –
albeit, for just a short time only – in Western Australia.
They were destined to become players in a horrific story
of mutiny and murder.[4]

Some of those left on the islands died of thirst before
rain brought fresh water. Perhaps they were the lucky ones.
They did not have to endure the reign of terror that was
imposed upon the survivors by Jeronimus Cornelisz.

Cornelisz was a psychopath with the ability to recruit
disciples. He quickly established himself as the leader of
the marooned community and sent the soldiers to look
for water on a nearby island. They were not allowed their
weapons. In the absence of the soldiers, Cornelisz and his
henchmen, apparently believing that Pelsaert would not
make it to Batavia, gave free reign to their worst impulses.
They raped the women and forced them into prostitution,
and murdered any men who opposed them. Roughly 120
people were murdered during Cornelisz's reign of terror.

A few men managed to escape from the island ruled
by Cornelisz and reached the soldiers, who had found

4 For a detailed account of the Batavia story see The Grey Company's website
at *http://members.iinet.net.au/~bill/batavia.html*

a good supply of fresh water. The soldiers, expecting Cornelisz to attack them, constructed fortifications and collected anything that could be used as weapons. Those fortifications have been preserved and are the oldest buildings in Australia.

Cornelisz and his followers did attack, but the soldiers succeeded in driving them back. Three attacks launched by Cornelisz were repelled. The third was in progress when Pelsaert arrived back from the Spice Islands. He took control of the situation and had the mutineers arrested. There was a trial and all those who had been guilty of criminal acts were sentenced: Cornelisz and a few of his most culpable followers were hung without delay; two others, who had not actually committed murder, were taken to the mainland and left there. The remaining men who had played a part in the killings were taken back to Batavia to be executed.

At least three more Dutch ships were later wrecked on the coast of Western Australia on the journey from Holland to the Spice Islands – the *Vergulde Draek* (1656), the *Zuytdorp* (1712) and the *Zeewijk* (1727).

The Dutch explorer who could be regarded as being most important in history of Western Australia was Willem de Vlamingh. In December 1696 he anchored his ship – the *Gellvinck* – in one of the bays of what he called Rattenest Island. That name he gave to the island because he thought that the quokkas there were extraordinarily large rats. From Rottnest – as the island is now known – he set out to explore the mainland. Rottnest was uninhabited, but as the Dutchmen ventured inland they came across a

primitive hut and a lot of footprints. The makers of these
footprints kept themselves well away from the foreign
invaders, so Vlamingh only caught a glimpse of them
in the distance. The Noongah people – the Australian
aboriginals who inhabited the area – were obviously not as
aggressive as those around the Gulf of Carpentaria who
had attacked the crew of the *Duyfken*.

Vlamingh explored and mapped what he named the
Black Swan River, as far inland as Heirisson Island. His
men managed to catch some of the swans. Black swans
were a novelty for Dutchmen, who had only ever seen
white ones. Perhaps it was as a result of Vlamingh's
explorations that the British later chose the Swan River as
a site for a settlement.

Neither the Dutch nor any other European nation
claimed title to any part of New Holland by occupation
until Governor Arthur Phillip raised the Union Jack at
Sydney Cove in 1788. At that stage the British were only
interested in the land east of longitude 135° east – the
eastern half of what was tentatively assumed to be an
island continent. The western half had been given such
a bad reputation by Dampier and the Dutch explorers
that neither Britain nor any other European country was
interested in claiming it.

Chapter 3: *Britain Claims The West*

By the second half of the eighteenth century the old maritime powers of Spain, Holland and Portugal had faded into relative insignificance. Britannia was ruling the waves and had become the dominant imperial power. The only serious challenger to Britain's supremacy was France. The French competed with Britain in claiming territory in North America and in the Caribbean, and they set up trading posts in Africa and colonies on Mauritius, Reunion and the Seychelles. The British East India Company faced fierce competition from the French East India Company in India.

After losing its thirteen colonies along the east coast of North America – due, in part, to the support France gave to the American rebels – Britain decided to establish the Colony of New South Wales. France was also interested in the South Pacific. While the First Fleet was in Botany Bay preparing to move to Port Jackson, a French ship, captained by Jean Francois de Galaup, *comte de Laperouse*, sailed into the Bay. Laperouse was in the course of an extensive journey of exploration around the rim of the

Pacific and had no intention of claiming territory for France. He was received courteously by the officers of the First Fleet and fortuitously entrusted to the British the records of his explorations to that point in his journey. Those records were sent back to Europe on the *Sirius*. Once the ship had been re-stocked with wood and water, Laperouse set sail again. His ship was lost at sea and there were no survivors.

Fear that the French might claim part of New Holland motivated the British to make a number of pre-emptive settlements around the coastline.

In 1804, Governor King, alarmed by the arrival of French ships on another voyage of exploration, sent a party of about fifty soldiers, sailors, settlers and convicts, to establish a settlement at Risdon Cove near the mouth of the Derwent River in Tasmania. The next year, convicts and settlers from England under the command of David Collins arrived to settle on the shores of Port Phillip to pre-empt any move by the French to claim what is now the State of Victoria. Collins decided that Port Phillip was not suitable and turned to King for advice. King suggested that Collins' party should join the settlers at Risdon Cove. Collins looked at Risdon Cove, but did not find it suitable, and instead established a new settlement at the foot of Mount Wellington, calling it Hobart.

To ensure that there could be no claim by the French that the north-east of the landmass was unoccupied, a convict settlement was established on the banks of the Brisbane River in 1824. The next year Britain formally claimed the area now called the Northern Territory and settlers were sent to establish a colony at Port Essington, about 150 kilometres north-east of Darwin. When they arrived, no reliable source of fresh water could be found, so the settlers instead went to Melville Island. Here they founded Fort Dundas. Fort Dundas was closed down after three years due to disease, lack of supplies and hostile indigenous people. Another settlement was then attempted at Raffles Bay on the Cobourg Peninsular in 1827. The settlers at Raffles Bay struck the same problems as had those at Fort Dundas and they left after just two years. A third attempt to occupy the far north was made in 1839. Port Essington was again chosen as the site. The new settlement survived for ten years until being ravaged by malaria and a cyclone. The Colony was eventually defeated and the settlers abandoned Port Essington for the second time.

In 1791 an English explorer, George Vancouver, discovered a superb deep-water harbour on the south coast of Western Australia. He named it King George Sound and formally claimed for the British Crown all of New Holland west of longitude 135° east. Ten years later Matthew Flinders dropped anchor in King George Sound in the course of his circumnavigation of Australia and spent a month there. King George Sound was subsequently chosen by Governor Darling as the site for a settlement to demonstrate to the French that Western Australia was a British possession.

On Christmas Day 1826 the brig *Amity* sailed into the Sound and entered the inner harbour, now known as Princess Royal Harbour. On board were a total of more than fifty men with some sheep, goats and other supplies calculated to be sufficient for six months. The passengers included the officer in charge, Major Edmund Lockyer, a surgeon, a storekeeper, eighteen soldiers and twenty three convicts, the ship's crew and four members of the Royal Navy. The settlement at Princess Royal Harbour was at first named Frederickstown to honour Prince Frederick, the Duke of York and Albany. It was renamed Albany by Governor James Stirling in 1831.

The settlers from the *Amity* were not the only Europeans in the area. Some seal hunters were living on islands not too far from King George Sound. Off the south coast there were a number of islands where seals were to be found. The small military establishment at King George Sound enjoyed a good relationship with the local indigenous Noongar people after Lockyer rescued young Noongar women that the seal hunters had kidnapped. He had the kidnappers arrested and sent back to Sydney to stand trial and he returned the women to their tribe. The Noongar were grateful and showed their gratitude by staging a corroboree at which the white men were honoured guests.

In 1827, Captain James Stirling set out to find another location in the west suitable for a settlement that would serve as a base for trading with the East Indies and to keep the French at bay. Stirling investigated the Swan River which had been first explored by Willem de Vlamingh about 130 years previously. Unlike those before him who had visited the area, Stirling was impressed by the Swan River as an area suitable for settlement. It was Stirling's opinion that the site on the north shore of the Swan River would be ideal for a town because just a few cannons positioned on Mount Eliza (named in honour of Eliza Darling, the wife of the governor) could easily defend it. Stirling was unconcerned by the fact that ships could not reach the place where he envisaged a town because the river mouth was blocked by rocks and a sand bar, nor was he worried that there was no deep-water harbour within hundreds of kilometres, or that the surrounding soil was unsuitable for agriculture.

Returning to England, Stirling campaigned for the establishment of a settlement of free citizens – with no convicts – on the banks of the Swan River. He had no fixed ideas about how his plans were to be achieved. At one stage he advocated that a company should be incorporated to control the new colony. Later he favoured an association such as the Quakers who had formed to establish Pennsylvania. The British Government eventually decided to establish a new colony under its direct control with Stirling as Lieutenant-Governor. To encourage investment in the proposed colony, a scheme was created under which individuals, syndicates and corporations would be granted land according to the amount of money they invested in fares and equipment.

The first ship to arrive at the Swan River with settlers was the *Challenger* under the command of Captain C. H. Fremantle. On 2 May 1829 he formally claimed all of New Holland outside the boundaries of New South Wales to be the new colony of Western Australia. It seemed that the settlement at King George Sound and the prior claim on the territory had been forgotten.

Stirling arrived four weeks later on the *Parmelia,* and *H M S Sulphur* arrived on 8 June. There was no harbour in which the three ships could shelter and they were unable to sail up the Swan River, so it was decided that they should anchor in Cockburn Sound where Garden Island provided some shelter from the swell of the Indian Ocean. The *Challenger* and the *Sulphur* both struck rocks in entering the Sound but suffered only minor damage. The *Parmelia* ran aground, sustaining damage to her keel and losing her rudder. She required major repairs. It was not an auspicious start for the new colony.

The settlers were off-loaded onto Garden Island where they and their possessions were exposed to harsh weather. Only Lieutenant Governor Stirling had waterproof accommodation. A pre-fabricated timber residence had been prepared for him in England and placed in the hold of one of the ships. It was assembled on the island and there Stirling lived in relative comfort until better accommodation was built for him on the mainland.

On 18 June Stirling proclaimed the foundation of the colony, but it was not until 27 July that this proclamation was circulated:

Notice is hereby given that on the 12th of August, the anniversary of the day on which His Gracious Majesty (King George the Fourth) was born, the first stone will be laid of a New Town to be called Perth, near the entrance to the estuary of the Swan River.
After that date the Public Business in the several Departments of Government will there be transacted,

and all applications for land, or on other subject,
received.
By the Command of His Excellency
P. Browne
Secretary to the Governor
The Office of the Secretary to Government, the
Surveyor of Territory, the Harbour Master, the Civil
Engineer and of the commissioners of the Board of
Counsel and Audit are to be opened for the despatch
of Business on the 12th day of next month at the points
indicated as the future site of the Town of Perth, where
a tent will be appropriated for each Department for
that purpose.[5]

On 12 August the occasion was marked not by the laying
of a stone but by the felling of a tree, near where the Perth
Town Hall now stands, by the wife of the captain of the
Sulphur, Mrs Helen Dance. By that stage some settlers had
been camped on Garden Island for over three months.

There is no doubt that the settlement of the Swan
River area was beset by more problems than most other
settlements in the early history of Australia except the
three failed colonies in the Northern Territory.

New immigrants arriving at the site of Perth found that
no preparations had been made for their settlement. The
area around Swam River had not been surveyed or even
properly explored. When parcels of land were eventually
distributed, the new owners had to clear it and construct
some form of shelter themselves. There was no convict
labour force to help them. The soil around the settlement

5 Cignet, 'The Birthplace of Perth', *Swan River Booklets,* vol 4, Paterson
Brokensha Pty Ltd, 1935, p13.

was too sandy for growing crops, and fresh water was hard to find. To make matters worse, under the system followed for the allocation of land those with the most invested in the enterprise were granted large areas close to the town. Those who had invested less were given smaller lots further out. There were no roads to the outlying allotments. Too much of the best land was granted to speculators who had no intention of development. It was all so chaotic that in 1867 Karl Marx cited the Swan River settlement as an example of the shortcomings of capitalism.

To add to those problems faced by the settlers, hostile Australian aboriginals were a threat – liable to steal from and even occasionally kill settlers. Clouds of mosquitoes came from the nearby swamps and the low-lying land near the river was liable to be flooded each winter. It was no wonder so many abandoned their plans to settle in Western Australia and instead migrated on to New South Wales. Joseph Hardey, a settler who arrived on the *Tranby* in February 1830, described the situation in a letter to a friend:

> *[We] found many of the emigrants in tents, at Fremantle, generally dissatisfied and full of complaints respecting the colony (and some of them ready for going away). The flats up the Swan, the badness of the soil, the heat of the weather, with many others things of the same kind, appeared to be the subjects of general conversation when worshipping at the shrine of Bacchus.[6]*

6 Western Australia Historical Society, *Early Days–Journals and Proceedings,* vol 3, reproduced by West Australian Newspapers, 1977, p63.

Stirling took responsibility for the survival of the colony upon himself, as had many of the early Governors of New South Wales from Phillip to Macquarie. While the settlers were struggling to clear their land and construct shelter, he ensured that starvation was avoided by purchasing food from South Africa and Van Diemen's Land. To find a reliable supply of fresh water, he sent an expedition to explore the Swan Valley. It came across a fresh water stream at a place they named Success Hill. Stirling had the town of Guildford established there. For some years Guildford, with its reliable supply of fresh water and better soil, was the main centre of the Swan River settlement.

In 1832 Stirling returned to England where he sought support for his struggling colony. He received no help and was even criticised for leaving his post without permission. But he was eventually knighted for his work in establishing the new outpost of the Empire and given the title Governor instead of just Lieutenant Governor.

Those who settled near the Swan River never enjoyed the sort of amiable relationship with the Australian aboriginals that existed at the small military settlement beside King George Sound. Hundreds of settlers moving in to claim title to traditional hunting grounds were bound to meet with resistance from the indigenous people. Stirling was unsympathetic to the idea that aboriginals had a prior right to the land. He did have a cordial relationship with those who were prepared to adapt to the presence of the settlers and he established an institute on Mount Eliza to educate aboriginal children. Any of the indigenous people who attacked or stole from the settlers he had arrested, put on trial and punished according to British law.

Some idea of the relationship between the Governor and the aboriginal people can be gathered from the *Manual for Emigrants*, published in 1839 by Nathaniel Ogle in which he stated that

> *'One chief, who with his son had been outlawed, asked for an interview with the governor and detailed the injuries his tribe had suffered, and sought a treaty of amity.'*[7]

The aboriginal who gave the setters the most trouble in the early years of the Swan River settlement was Yagan. He was identified as the leader of a series of attacks against white settlers along the Canning River. He and some of his fellow guerrillas were captured and taken to Carnac Island – a small island about a kilometre north of Garden Island. There Robert Lyon attempted to teach them how to live in a civilised community. Yagan was not interested. He stole a boat, made his way back to the mainland, and was soon stealing from the settlers again. After he led an attack on some carts taking provisions to settlers along the Canning River during which the drivers of the carts were speared to death, a reward was offered for his capture.

On 11 July 1833 two young lads, William and James Yates, were minding cattle when Yagan and a number of other armed aboriginals appeared. William shot Yagan and James shot another of the group. The two boys had no time to re-load and they ran for their lives. William

7 N Ogle, *The Colony of Western Australia,* James Fraser, London, 1839, p50.

was speared to death, but James – aged just 13 – managed to escape. Later, a group of settlers discovered the scene of the battle and cut off Yagan's head so that it could be produced as evidence of his death and that the reward could be collected.[8]

Yagan was highly regarded by Robert Lyon. In an article in the *Perth Gazette* Lyon likened him to the Scottish leader William Wallace, who fought against English occupation of Scotland in the thirteenth century.

While Stirling was in England his deputy, Captain Frederick Irwin, treated the Australian aboriginals harshly and relationships between the settlers and the aboriginals deteriorated. One tribe, the Binjareb, proved to be particularly aggressive. They had an audacious leader called Calyute. Calyute led a raid on the mill in South Perth and stole half a ton of flour. He was captured, publicly flogged and imprisoned for a few months. Soon after he had been released he led another attack, this time on the property of Thomas Peel at Mandurah during which one servant was killed and another injured.

Stirling returned to the colony in 1834 in time to deal with Calyute. A small army of police and settlers were assembled, and Stirling led them to find and punish those responsible for the attack on Peel's property.

On 28 October the posse surrounded the Binjareb campsite near the Murray River, close to the location of what is now Pinjarra. The confrontation between attackers

---

8 Yagan's head was taken to a museum in England. After a century or so it was buried in an unmarked grave. Aboriginal activists campaigned for its return, and in 1997 it was exhumed and sent back to Perth to be buried with his body in a memorial park beside the Great Northern Highway. A statue of Yagan was erected on Heirisson Island in 1984. The publicity given to the return of Yagan's head inspired someone to cut the head off the statue. It was replaced, and that head too was cut off. Neither head has ever been recovered.

with firearms and defenders with spears was predictably one-sided. What has been called the 'Battle of Pinjarra' was soon over. It was said by the settlers that 60 to 80 aboriginals were in the camp and that the number killed was as few as 11 or as many as 40. Just one police officer was among the casualties. Some indigenous Australians have since claimed that more than 100 died. The incident has been described as a massacre rather than a battle.

Calyute, however, managed to escape. In May 1840 he led an attack on a Noongar camp near Perth in which five were speared. To this day, nothing else is known about him.

Stirling persevered with governing the Swan River settlement until October 1837. The settlement had clearly not been the success he had hoped. After almost ten years the European population of Western Australia numbered only about three thousand. Those planning a different approach for the settlement of South Australia held the Swan River Colony up as an example of how not to establish a colony of free settlers.

Chapter 4: *Thomas Peel*

The story of Thomas Peel was cited by critics of the Swan River enterprise as the prime example of all that was wrong with the planning of the Swan River colony.

Peel was a wealthy attorney who, in 1828, intended to immigrate to New South Wales, but reconsidered when he heard of proposals for a new colony in Western Australia. He became involved in an association that was being formed to sponsor settlers for the proposed colony. The association planned to recruit ten thousand settlers over a four year period and place them on 200 acre allotments in the colony. In return for its part in establishing the new colony, the association hoped to be granted four million acres of good land.

The association's scheme was submitted to the British Government but was rejected. The government, influenced by Stirling, decided that it was not going to give the Swan River settlement over to private enterprise. At that point the members of the Association – with the exception of Peel – lost interest.

Peel then entered into a partnership with Solomon Levey to take advantage of what they imagined would be an opportunity to make a fortune from investing in the proposed colony. Levey was a former convict who had amassed a fortune while living in New South Wales. He was not likely to successfully appeal to the members of the British Government, so it was decided that Levey's role would remain undisclosed.

Peel negotiated with the Colonial Office, and an agreement was reached under which he was to be granted 250,000 acres initially, and a further 250,000 when he had brought 400 settlers to the colony. Subject to the fulfilment of conditions regarding improvements on that first 500,000 acres, he would be granted a further 500,000. Peel marked on a map the area he wanted; a stretch of land beside the Canning River, not far from where Stirling had envisaged the capital of the colony. The government promised that area would be his if he and 400 of his settlers arrived at the colony before 1 November 1829. The conditions the British Government placed upon the land grants to Peel's settlers were set out clearly in a document dated 5 December 1828.[9]

When Peel advised his wife that they would be soon leaving for Western Australia, her response was to state that she was pregnant and her child was going to be delivered in England. Peel decided to leave her behind, and instead take their eleven year old son, Frederick, with him. In the will he signed before leaving England, Peel described Frederick as 'my reputed son'. Perhaps he was not absolutely certain that he was in fact the boy's father.

9 Historical Records of Australia, vol. 4, p394.

Peel left himself little time to spare when he departed from London for Plymouth where he was to join the ship that would take him to Western Australia. To make matters worse, the ship – the *Gilmore* – pulled into Plymouth harbour over a week behind schedule. The captain, William Geary, reported to Peel that his crew had mutinied during the short voyage from London and were refusing to sail with him to Australia. Peel wasted time seeking a court order to force the members of the crew to fulfil their agreement to sail. The crew did not just wait in Plymouth to be served with a writ. A new crew had to be found. Peel wrote to Sir George Murray, Secretary of State for the Colonies, asking for an extension of time. No extension of time was granted before the *Gilmore* set sail for the Swan River.

Before the ship arrived at Capetown, Captain Geary proposed to one of his lady passengers and she agreed to marry him. The *Gilmore* remained docked in Capetown while its captain made arrangements for the wedding. The wedding was celebrated and he and his bride had a brief honeymoon before the ship continued to Western Australia.

Meanwhile, at the Swan River a number of immigrants were enviously eyeing the prime land being kept for Peel. Stirling advised them that it was being kept available for Thomas Peel, provided he arrived to claim it by 1 November. When that date passed and Peel had not appeared, Stirling granted the land to waiting settlers. He had received from the Colonial Office this instruction:

The governor is not to put Mr Peel on the Council. If, as is probable, his party shall arrive too late for fulfilment

of the conditions on which he received his grant, he will
have no claim at all; and even if he arrives on time I
cannot but think that the impetuosity and indiscretion,
to use no harsher words, which he has betrayed in his
communication with this department, will render him
an unsafe member of a Body whose deliberations are
likely to involve both general and individual interests
of great and yearly increasing importance.[10]

Peel and 179 immigrants arrived six weeks after the
date by which he had to claim the land he had wanted.
Stirling advised him that the area had been re-allocated to
others. Peel promptly returned to the *Gilmore* and ordered
Captain Geary to prepare to sail back to England, though
Geary had no desire to sail for England at that stage. The
Hobart newspaper *Colonial Times,* which had a keen interest
in what was happening over at the Swan River, reported
that *'It appears that a duel was fought between Mr Peel and*
the Commander of the vessel in which that gentleman came
passenger'.[11] There is no other evidence that a duel was
fought, but duelling was illegal and the parties involved
in the duel between Peel and Geary – if there was one –
would have been reluctant to talk about it.

Stirling, in an effort to prevent Peel from slandering the
colony, and to keep his putative 400 settlers, invited Peel
to accompany him on an inspection of an alternative site
where Peel and his immigrants might settle. They rode
some ten kilometres south of Fremantle to Woodman
Point where, Stirling claimed, a new town to be called
'Clarence' was planned. Stirling promised that Peel's

10   Colonial Office documents 18/3 p. 31.
11   The Colonial Times, April 2, 1830.

settlers could be the foundation citizens of what would be an important port for the Canning River district.

Woodman Point was far from being the ideal location for a new settlement.Cockburn Sound was not a natural harbour. The water was shallow, without shelter for moorings, and became rough in bad weather. The soil where the town of Clarence was to be located was sand strewn with limestone rocks, and the stunted vegetation was thick. It was a long way from Fremantle and even further from Perth. Despite the obvious disadvantages of the site, Peel agreed to base his immigrants there. Three weeks after arriving in Western Australia, they were set ashore near Woodman Point.

Peel's settlers camped in the sand hills and work was started on a survey of the proposed town. The survey was never completed and the idea of the town of Clarence never came to fruition.

The migrants did what they could to provide themselves with some form of shelter where they guessed or hoped their grant might be. Peel and his son occupied a 'residence' more substantial than most – the stall that had been on the *Gilmore* to accommodate his horse on the journey to the colony.

On 13 February the ship *Hooghly* arrived with 173 more settlers, and they were also set ashore at Woodman Point. Three days later a bush fire – said to have been started by aboriginals – swept towards the area where Peel's immigrants were living. Some lost their tent homes and many of their possessions. Peel came to the conclusion that the area was just not suitable and he set off in the brig

Industry to look for better land further south. He became convinced that the land around the entrance of the Murray was better than the Clarence town site, and sent a group of men to prepare the foundations of a settlement.

Before Peel could claim his first 250,000 acres, he had to have landed at least 400 settlers in the colony. The ship bringing the last of the arrivals was the *Rockingham*. She finally appeared off the coast of Western Australia on 12 May 1830, just in time for one of Perth's winter storms. For two days she rode out the storm and then attempted to enter Cockburn Sound. Battling strong winds and a rough surf, she managed to approach Woodman Point where the anchor was dropped. However, the wind was too strong and the ship's capstan broke. With no way of preventing his ship being carried along by the wind, the captain decided to head further into the Sound where the ship finally ran aground at Mangles Bay. Peel had a reputation for being touchy and hot-tempered. It had already been reported that he had previously fought a duel with the captain of the *Gilmore*, and it was said that he also fought a duel with Captain Halliburton, the master of the *Rockingham*. Whether or not there was a duel, Peel incurred an extremely severe wound to his right hand. He was incapacitated for weeks and, it was reported, was fortunate not to have to undergo an amputation. The *Swan River Guardian* later claimed that '*Mr. Peel at this period betook himself to Garden Island and entirely forsook his people, leaving instructions that nothing was to be done without his written order. He gave no written order.*'[12] He claimed to have incurred the wound while out shooting.

12 *The Swan River Guardian*, March 18. 1837.

Peel expected that his settlers would be provided with supplies that Levey would arrange to be sent from Sydney. Some did arrive but it was far from adequate, and local authorities were obliged to step in to supply the colonists with some food. They held Peel personally responsible for the cost. It was not until 1851 that Peel was finally able to shed the burden of his debt to the Colonial Government.

The health of the settlers at the town of Clarence had deteriorated so much over the winter of 1829 that Stirling sent Alexander Collie – the surgeon from H.M.S. *Sulphur* – to investigate. Collie reported that scurvy and dysentery were the worst problems, caused by poor diet and brackish water. He noted that the settlers lacked both the equipment for fishing – their best source of fresh food – and the initiative to make such equipment for themselves. Twenty nine settlers died at Woodman Point during the summer in 1830.

Peel's migrants were, for a time, supported financially by promissory notes issued by the Sydney firm of Cooper and Levey. However, when Levey's health seriously declined, his partner – Cooper – decided to no longer honour the notes. Disheartened, many of Peel's migrants abandoned their plans to be part of Peel's settlement project, choosing instead to look for paid work. Peel sued those who left the initiative for the cost of their passage out to the colony and in return they sued him for their wages. Peel was involved in a considerable amount of litigation.

Peel moved down to the land he had chosen beside the estuary of the Murray River. Though he had no title to the land he occupied he built a small three-room cottage and named it Mandurah House. Some of his immigrants moved from Woodman Point to join him. For a time Peel showed some interest in those who were still living at the site of the town of Clarence. The Colonial Storekeeper, John Morgan, noted in a letter to a friend at the Colonial Office:

The Proprietor of a million acres of land – one of the founders of what may be hereafter a mighty nation – is now to be seen driving with the assistance only of his son (a lad about fifteen years of age) his two horse team between the Murray and Clarence, or plodding along upon a miserable half-starved pony, and without a shilling in his pocket anxiously thinking how he is to manage the purchase of his next month's daily food.[13]

Those remaining at Clarence gradually departed from that bleak area. There is now nothing at Woodman Point to demonstrate that once over 500 people lived there.

Most of the colonists who did move to Mandurah did not stay with Peel for long. The aboriginals of the Murray River area were numerous and unpredictable. The murder of one of Peel's servants resulted in the Battle of Pinjarra and after this the remaining settlers deserted him for Perth.

Peel had only his son and a few servants for company until two other pioneers moved into the area. Francis Byrne also took up land near the mouth of the Murray River and became one of Peel's few allies. Byrne represented Peel

13 From Swan River Papers – transcripts of Colonial Office documents in Western Australian archives 15/71

in court when Peel was unable to be present, and Peel appointed Byrne as an executor of his estate. Edward Hall built a cottage on the southern side of the entrance to the estuary – the area now known as Hall's Head.

Levey died in 1833, depriving Peel of his only source of financial support.

In 1834 Peel's wife arrived in the colony, bringing with her two daughters – Dorothy aged seven and Julia aged thirteen – and her son Thomas aged nine. She also brought a huge amount of luggage – 22 pieces in all, including a piano. Peel's three-roomed cottage with a floor of stamped earth must have been a disappointment to her. The Reverend John Wollaston visited Peel in 1842, and he described Mandurah House as a *'despicable hut, or nest of huts, built of stone and covered (not thatched) with rushes.'* Regarding Peel he added:

> Everything about him shows the broken-down gentleman; clay floors and handsome plate, curtains for doors and a pianoforte, windows without glass and costly china, hardly any utensil put to its proper use, odd cups and saucers ... the only looking glass the size of a hand and a whole pig hanging in the verandah.[14]

Within a couple of months Peel was forced to write to the Colonial Secretary to ask for the money to return his family to England:

> My only wish now is to get my family away, either to the Cape or to any other part from which they can

14   JR Wollaston, Wollaston's Picton Journal, C.H Pitman and Sons, 1948, p60.

proceed to England. To see them suffer as they have every prospect, I cannot endure. I therefore would gladly undergo any sacrifice or personal suffering to promote their return to England.[15]

The Colonial Secretary was no help, but at least Peel's title to the land he had occupied – 250,000 acres – was granted in fee simple. He then applied for the promised second grant of 250,000 acres, but was refused.

In 1839 Peel managed to sell 13,770 acres, enabling him to clear some of his debts and send his wife and two daughters back to England where he hoped soon to join them. Young Thomas remained in Mandurah with his father and Frederick. Unfortunately Peel was unable to find buyers for any large part of his land and was so forced to remain in the colony burdened by debt.

In 1851, Levey's heir, John Levey Roberts (he had adopted the surname of his mother) came to Western Australia to finalise his father's dealings with Peel. Enough of the Murray River land was sold to pay off the debts incurred by Peel on behalf of the partnership, and the remaining land was equally divided between Peel and Roberts. Peel then held just over 100,000 acres near what is now called the Peel Inlet.

Still poor and having little more to his name than his unproductive real estate, Peel never did join his wife back in England. His elder daughter died of tuberculosis in London in 1856 and his wife died of the same disease the next year. His younger daughter, Dorothy, then came back to Western Australia to live with him.

15 A Hasluck, *Thomas Peel of Swan River*, Oxford University Press, Melbourne, 1965, p148.

As he grew older, Peel became poorer and more eccentric. He was often seen riding around his large property wearing a faded, old red hunting coat, perhaps living out a fantasy of being an English gentleman. He died at Mandurah in 1865 and was buried in the churchyard there. His land was divided into three parcels and inherited by Thomas, Dorothy and Frederick.

It should be mentioned that Peel's was not the only privately sponsored immigration scheme. Colonel Peter Laurtour promoted a less ambitious scheme, under which he sponsored 85 settlers in Fremantle in August 1829. They remained in Fremantle until suitable land was found for them. Over 100,000 acres was allotted to Laurtour's settlers. His scheme did not proceed smoothly, but it attracted little of the sort of adverse publicity that Peel's did. He himself never immigrated to Western Australia.

Chapter 5: *The Dispersion*

The colony needed land suitable for growing cereals to feed the increasing number of immigrants. In 1829, Stirling ordered Ensign Robert Dale to lead a small exploration party up and over the Darling escarpment that overlooks the coastal plain and, if possible, find some land suitable for growing wheat.

Dale followed the course of the Swan River inland. At one point the river divided, and the tributary that the party decided to explore came to be known as the Avon River. Following it, they came to the area where the town of Northam now stands. They then continued on to reach the sites of what are now York and Beverley.

It was the York site that was selected to be the place for Western Australia's first inland town. Settlers arrived in September 1831 and were successful in growing wheat and barley. Within a few years the town of York had begun to take shape. It received a boost when an army barracks and store were constructed and a contingent of soldiers arrived to protect the settlers. York became the departure point for pastoralists, sandalwood cutters and explorers setting out for the flat, drier inland areas.

Encouraged by the success of York, settlers trekked up the Swan and Avon valleys and began farming at Northam in 1833. The site for another town in what is now known as the Wheatbelt was surveyed in 1831. It was to be named Beverley, although settlers did not arrive there until 1860.

The settlements expanded eastwards slowly because the rainfall declines sharply as one moves away from the south-western corner of the state. When all the best land around the Swan River had been allocated and immigrants continued to arrive, Governor Stirling had to look further afield for areas where he could locate the new arrivals.

In March 1830 the *Warrior* reached Western Australia with a number of settlers as passengers including the Bussell brothers and the Turner, Molloy, Layman and Chapman families. Stirling suggested that they would all be well advised to move on and settle further south.

In April 1830 Stirling went with the Bussells, Molloys, Laymans, Turners and Chapmans to find a suitable site for a satellite settlement near the Blackwood River, at the extreme southwest of Western Australia. The settlers were happy with the land offered to them there, and the town of Augusta – named after a daughter of King George IV – was established. The total population of the Augusta district was about thirty, and that included the Turners' seven children and a small detachment of soldiers.

From Augusta, John Bussell went exploring northwards and he came to Geographe Bay. He recognised that the land around the bay was better for farming than the land around Augusta. In 1834 Bussell moved his family to the Geographe Bay area and there they prospered by raising cattle on a property named *Cattle Chosen*. Within a few years most of the Augusta settlers had moved north to join them. Many settled near Wonnerup where the original homestead built by the Layman family in 1838 and the school built in 1874 have been well preserved as tourist attractions.

The land around Wonnerup is low-lying and inclined to turn marshy, so the main town was developed a few kilometres further south. It was officially named 'Busselton' in 1835 – not surprisingly, since John Bussell had pioneered settlement of the area and the number of Bussells there almost doubled when his brother, Lennox, and his sisters, Frances and Bessie immigrated from England to join him.

Of all those who pioneered the settlements at Augusta and Geographe Bay, perhaps the most celebrated – other than John Bussell – are John Molloy and his wife Georgiana. John Molloy was appointed the resident magistrate for the area and continued in that role until old age prevented him from doing so, while pioneering the settlement of the Vasse area. Georgiana was the archetype of the tough pioneer woman, and in the most remote settlement in Australia, gave birth to five daughters who survived her and a son who drowned when just eighteen months old. Her husband was often away on his duties as a magistrate so she managed the family and farm on her own. In 1836 she received a letter from the botanist James Mangles asking her to collect specimens of the local flora for him. That initiated an intense interest in botany and she became a well-regarded self-taught botanist. Her pressed specimens and the seeds she collected were highly valued in England, and horticulturalists were able to grow plants from her seeds. After the birth of her last child – her fifth daughter – she was unable to recover her strength. The birth had been difficult and according to the Anglican clergyman John Wollaston, who ministered to her in her last days, the doctor was drunk. For three months she hardly left her bed and eventually died in 1843. One of her daughters married Matthew Blagden Hale, the first Anglican Bishop of Western Australia and the Anglican school in Busselton is called the 'Georgiana Molloy Anglican School'.

Three other small settlements were established between the Swan River and Busselton around the Leschanault Inlet while Stirling was governor. The inlet had been given that name by the French explorer Nicolas Baudin who visited the area in 1801. Leschenault de la Tour was that expedition's botanist. Stirling decided to place a military base near the mouth of the Collie River in order to ward off any claim by the French should they return. The town established there he named 'Bunbury'

In 1831 Stirling also reserved for a future township an area inland from Bunbury near a ford that allowed people to cross the Murray River. Settlers did not arrive there until six years later. The town – named Pinjarra after the aboriginal tribe (the Pindjarup) that lived in the area – is near where the Battle of Pinjarra was fought.

A company called the Western Australian Company was formed in England in 1840 to sell land on the Leschanault Inlet and establish a town to be called Australind. The company's operations did not proceed smoothly. The location of the site was changed and the company's bankers failed, but the first shipload of almost one hundred settlers left England in December that year. The natural leader of that group was a Mr Clifford who was accompanied by his wife and eleven children. Clifford proudly claimed theirs was the first settlement in British history to be established without the support of any naval, military or civil authority. Unfortunately the Australind settlement did not prosper. At its peak the population of the settlement reached about 350. By the end of 1846 it was down to about 70 and the company was forced to abandon the project. It seems that the lots allocated to each settler were too small to enable them to make a living, there were no markets nearby for their produce and many of the settlers were not the type to be pioneers.[16]

From Albany some Europeans also ventured north-wards into the hinterland. In 1829, Dr T.B. Wilson, with an aboriginal guide, came across the Hay River. There, near to a prominent hill that came to be known as Mount Barker, he found fertile soil and a good supply of fresh water. In 1831 Dr Alexander Collie, again guided by an aboriginal, discovered good land where the town of Kendenup now stands just a few kilometres north of Mount Barker. There he took up a holding of 5,000 acres. Other settlers, the most notable of which were George Cheyne, John Morley, William Preston and Thomas Bannister, followed those pioneers into the Mount Barker area. The rate of settlement of the land north of Albany increased after 1835 when Governor Stirling and the Surveyor-General, J.S. Roe, explored the route from Albany to where the

---

16   Western Australia Historical Society, *The Settlement at Australind* in Early Days, vol 3 of Western Australian Historical Society, p23 et seq.

town of Williams – over 400 kilometres north of Albany – was later established.

As the settled areas of the colony spread over a vast area, Stirling wrote to the authorities in England requesting more soldiers for protection from attacks by aboriginals. In his letter he stated:

It is necessary to observe that the population is scattered over a very wide extent of the country... Having the power to select large grants in districts suitable to their views the settlers naturally avail themselves of their freedom of choice; and lands being subject to forfeiture if not improved within a certain number of years, they have been impelled by fear of losing them to locate themselves upon their grounds, however remote their position. This dispersion has been further increased by the nature of the country in respect of its general infertility of soil or the absence of water in certain localities.[17]

**  **

The movement of settlers into the area east of Albany known as the Eucla did not begin until the late 1860's. One of the first pioneers of the area, John Dunn, was said to have been a seal hunter when he first visited where the town of Hopetoun is now situated. He set to work clearing land and installing the facilities he would need for a farm. With his brother George, he went to Albany

17   GH Burvill, *Agriculture in Western Australia 1829-1979*, University of Western Australia Press, p6.

in 1871 and purchased sheep. It took them about three months to drive their flock to their station, which they had named Cocanarup. In 1873 John Dunn was granted title to the land he had occupied, but he did not have long to enjoy it. He was killed by aboriginals in 1880.

John Dunn's brother, James, discovered gold at nearby Annabel Creek, and that led to the establishment of the town of Ravensthorpe. Writing in her diary on 25 September 1885, an Albany resident, Kate Keyser, noted:

Heard very bad news from the Phillips River. Natives attacked the Dunn Brothers there and had beaten James Dunn and left him for Dead, his brother Robert was also attacked by them, but he shot 2 of them and wounded three more. It is a very sad Affair, as there Brother John was killed at the same Place by the Natives.[18]

Venturing further east, the Dempster family established a sheep station in the 1870s near where the town of Esperance was later developed. Poor soil inhibited the development of that area until the 1960s when the country was made more productive by introducing trace elements and fertilisers. Until then, Esperance was primarily a port serving the miners of the Eastern Goldfields.

18 J Dowson, *Old Albany*, Albany Chamber of Commerce and Industry, 2008.

Chapter 6:

Northward And The Pastoralists

At first the dispersion did not take many settlers north of Perth. The coastal plain for some distance northwards is generally not good for farming, and beyond the suburbs still remains sparsely populated.

The discovery of good farming land further north was the incidental result of an attempt by a party led by George Grey to explore the coastline between North West Cape and Shark Bay. In 1839, an American whaler conveyed the explorers – and the three boats in which they intended to travel – to Bernier Island at Shark Bay. In crossing from there to the mainland during rough weather one of the boats and most of their supplies were lost. Grey abandoned his idea of going north, and the party set out to return to Perth in the remaining two boats. At Gantheaume Bay near the mouth of the Murchison River their two remaining boats were wrecked. The explorers were faced with having to walk back to Perth – some 480 kilometres – with no supplies. All but one of the explorers managed to survive.

Grey reported that the land through which he had trekked was suitable for agriculture and pastoral activity. In 1846, Augustus Charles Gregory was given command of an expedition to further explore the area through which Grey had passed. He found good grazing land and a seam of coal at the Irwin River. Two years later he went north again and mapped the course of the Murchison River and found traces of lead.

It was mining – not the search for land on which to settle – that first brought the British to what became known as the Champion Bay district. The Geraldine Mining Company was formed in Perth to exploit the lead deposits Gregory had discovered. The first mine the company attempted was unwisely situated in the dry bed of the Murchison River. While some lead ore was extracted by convicts and shipped out of Port Gregory (40 kilometres from where Geraldton was later established) the Murchison suddenly filled with water. The mine was moved to the north-west bank and, for a time, the Geraldine Mining Company made a worthwhile profit. A fall in the price of lead resulted in the Geraldine mine becoming unprofitable – despite the free convict labour – and it was closed down.

Miners in Northampton discovered copper and exceptionally high-grade lead ore which was exported through the port of Geraldton, which had been officially gazetted as a town in 1850. A railway line was constructed from Northampton to Geraldton, a distance of about 53 kilometres. That was the first Government railway to be built in the colony. A private line for hauling timber had previously been built near Busselton.

Farmers and graziers began to move into the area in 1849. That year William and Lockier Burges selected the Bowes Estate (48,000 hectares) near Northampton. The next year there was a severe drought in the Wheatbelt and many farmers moved north to the rich alluvial flats of the Irwin, Greenough and Chapman Rivers. Away from the flats a number of stations such as White Peak, Minnenooka and Tibraddeen were established as pastoral holdings. By 1859 there were almost one thousand settlers, over 43,000 sheep and 4,000 cattle in the Champion Bay district. That population quadrupled over the next ten years, as did the stock numbers.

Pastoralists in low rainfall areas depending upon the natural vegetation to sustain their flocks or herds needed large areas of land in order to make a living. Few – if any – of the pioneer pastoralists in Western Australia could afford to buy the amount of real estate they needed. The British Government determined the price at which Crown land was to be sold, and the Colonial Office clearly did not appreciate the real value of land in the Australian colonies. In 1830 it increased the minimum price of Crown land in all parts of the Colony of New South Wales from five shillings per acre to twelve shillings per acre, making the minimum price for barren land west of Bourke the same as land in the fertile river valleys along the coast.

It was a common practice for settlers in Western Australia to buy a small area on which to build a home and grow crops, and then allow their sheep or cattle to graze on nearby Crown land. By 1845 in the Moore River area at least six graziers had out-stations and there were about eight flocks each of about 2,000 sheep grazing on Crown land in the region.

John Hutt, who succeeded Stirling as Governor of Western Australia, decided to put an end to this practice of pastoralists making use of Crown land without paying to do so. He established the system of Pastoral Leases. Under that system pastoralists had to negotiate leases from the government if they wished to graze stock on Crown land. Anyone guilty of grazing stock on land for which they did not have a valid lease was prosecuted for trespass.

To this day, pastoral leases granted in Western Australia are subject to strict special conditions. The holder may only use the property leased for pastoral purposes and is not permitted to cultivate the land in any way. Any holder of a pastoral lease who grows a crop there may be penalised. The land has to be used in an environmentally sound way and no exotic plants may be introduced. Improvements required to be made to the property and numbers of stock to be grazed are usually specified. The lease cannot be sold without government approval.

**  **

The movement of settlers into the Pilbara – that is, the area between the Tropic of Capricorn and the Great Sandy Desert – followed Francis Gregory's explorations in 1861. He reported that the area was suitable for pastoral activity, and within two years Walter Padbury and John Wellard had arrived at the area where the town of Cossack was later established, bringing substantial flocks of sheep. Other settlers arrived, and by 1869 there were over 39,000 sheep in the Pilbara.

For a time, Cossack was the Pilbara's most important port. It was the gateway to the pastoral country and the gold mines at Marble Bar, and a base for pearl fishers. When the harbour at Cossack became contaminated by silt, the pearl fishers moved to Broome, and the nearby Port Samson became the major port for the area. Cossack became a ghost town. Roebourne – established in 1866 – became the most important coastal centre and remained so until a railway was built from Marble Bar to Port Hedland in 1912.

The port of Onslow was developed in 1883 to service the Ashburton River area south of Cossack. However, it was built in an unsheltered area prone to severe cyclones. After most of the buildings in the town had been severely damaged a number of times by winds up to 232 kilometres per hour, the town was moved some twenty kilometres to a more sheltered area.

The area known as the Kimberley north of the Great Sandy Desert sparked interest as a pastoral belt when Alexander Forrest explored the district in 1879. Forrest set himself up as a land agent specialising in the area. His newspaper advertisement stated:

Having had more than eleven years experience in Crown land transactions, and having an intimate

*knowledge of nearly the whole of Western Australia,
he is prepared to select and arrange the boundaries of
any lands required; to arrange for payment of rents;
undertake sales of estates and leases; to negotiate
loans and mortgages; to report on, survey and value
properties, and generally to transact all business
connected with land.*[19]

His glowing accounts of the potential of the Kimberley
were noted with interest by a number of men in the
eastern states, including the Duracks, Solomon Emanuel
and Charles Macdonald.

Patrick Durack was born in County Clare, Ireland, and
migrated to Australia in 1853. He settled in Goulburn
where he befriended Solomon Emanuel, a banker and
pastoralist, then went to the Victorian goldfields to make
his fortune. After 18 months of prospecting, he returned
with enough capital to finance the purchase of a farm.
However, he found life on a small farm dissatisfying. With
his brother Michael and brother-in-law John Costello
he went to establish a cattle station in south-western
Queensland. Their cattle perished in a severe drought,
but they managed to profit from land speculation. By
1879 Patrick Durack was a wealthy man – the owner of
hotels, a considerable area of land, and large herds of
cattle and flocks of sheep – and Costello had retired to
live on the coast.

Durack then read Alexander Forrest's promotion of
the land in the Kimberley. He and his friend Solomon
Emanuel financed an expedition in 1882, led by Michael

19 J Nairn, *Western Australia's Tempestuous History*, vol 2, North Stirling Press,
Perth, 1877, p15.

Durack, to ascertain the potential of the area for pastoral exploitation. Michael's favourable report decided Patrick Durack to take up land near the Ord River and Emanuel to invest in property near the Fitzroy River.

Durack decided to stock his holding with cattle from his Queensland station, and organized over 7,000 cattle to be driven from south Queensland to the far north of Western Australia – a distance of nearly 5,000 kilometres. The drive took two years and four months. About half the cattle and some of his drovers died along the way. He lived on his station near the Ord River for just a few years before selling up and retiring to Brisbane. Two of his sons then set up the Argyle Downs Station beside the Behn River. Durack returned to the Kimberley to live at Argyle Downs when his financial dealings in Brisbane turned sour, and died in Fremantle in 1898.

The Durack family did have luck on their side. The discovery of gold at Hall's Creek in 1885 led to the establishment of a port – Wyndham – not far from their holdings. When the gold was mined out and the Hall's Creek township shrank to a tiny settlement, Wyndham became virtually the Durack's own port.

Fossil Downs, the largest privately owned cattle station in Australia – nearly 405,000 hectares – was established by Charles Macdonald. He had his cattle driven from Laggan near Goulbourn to the Victoria River, a trek of over 5,800 kilometres. It was a longer drive than that undertaken by the Duracks, yet it took just eleven months.

The story of the settlement at Camden Sound should be told – even though it was a complete fiasco – because visiting the ruins of the buildings there is one of the highlights of the popular tours of the Kimberley coast.

In 1864, a convict named Wildman claimed to have found gold in the Kimberley. He said that he had been a member of the crew of a Dutch ship in 1856 when it was forced to land for repairs. He reported that he had wandered off into the countryside, had come across a rich gold reef and had collected a number of nuggets that he had later sold in Liverpool for 416 pounds. He volunteered to lead an official party to the site of his find if granted a remission of part of his sentence.

At first Wildman was disbelieved, but a rumour spread that checks in Liverpool had verified the fact that nuggets had been sold there for exactly the price Wildman had reported. The governor consented to releasing Wildman in order to lead the expedition. Wildman set off for the Kimberley on the schooner *New Perseverance* with eight men, horses and provisions – all supplied by the government.

When the party landed at Camden Sound, Wildman suddenly refused to cooperate. The others went off to search for gold, but found nothing. Wildman was returned to the gaol in Fremantle.

Two other expeditions went north, hoping to find Wildman's reef. All they found was trouble with hostile aboriginals. Three explorers were speared to death and an unknown number of aboriginals were shot.

Some misleading reports that explorers had found good pastoral country in the Camden Sound area gained currency in Melbourne. The Camden Pastoral Association Limited was incorporated with the stated objective of settling what was claimed to be superior, well-watered pastoral country at Camden Sound. Its prospectus alleged that the Association had the right to lease four million acres. By the end of 1864 seventy three shareholders had agreed to take up land at Camden Sound and the first group arrived there in December with their families, possessions and stock.

In a scene reminiscent of the first settlers arriving at Garden Island, the Camden Sound settlers and their possessions were off-loaded onto the beach. Without any shelter and in the high temperatures of mid-summer, supplies were ruined and stock perished as the area had little in the way of pasture or drinkable water. Some of the stock that had survived was poisoned by native vegetation. By the end of the first two months, three quarters of the animals brought by the settlers had died.

Two more shiploads of settlers arrived to exacerbate an already desperate situation. A supply ship, the *Calliance,* struck a reef while entering the harbour and sank. By the end of February 1865 three quarters of the settlers – those who could afford to pay for the passage back to Melbourne – had left. The rest did what they could to make the best of their situation, but the settlement was doomed. The governor, John Hampton, finally came to the rescue of those trapped at Camden Sound, allowing them to exchange their leases there for leases of land near Cossack. All that remains as evidence of the failed settlement is a graveyard on a small island.

Chapter 7: *Convicts*

In 1837, a committee was set up by the House of Commons
to enquire into the effectiveness of transportation as a
punishment and a means by which offenders might be
rehabilitated. It concluded that transportation was not the
best way to deal with criminals and should be discontinued.
In 1840 Governor Gipps advised the Legislative Council
of New South Wales that the British Government would
be sending no more convicts to Sydney. That news
was greeted with delight by a substantial sector of the
population of New South Wales. An anti-transportation
movement within the colony had considerable support.
Its members considered convicts to be depriving honest
workers of opportunities to find work. The movement
also believed that convicts were a source of crime and
therefore a stain on the reputation of a colony in which,
by then, the majority of the population were immigrants
with no criminal record.

For a few years no criminals were transported to Australia.
The prisons in England became seriously overcrowded. In
1849 it was decided to send more convicts to New South Wales.

The barque *Hashemy* set sail for Australia from Portsmouth in February of that year carrying 212 male convicts, 29 of whom were just young boys. Sixteen of the boys died during the voyage. The surviving boys were put ashore at Port Phillip, and the *Hashemy* proceeded to Sydney where she was greeted by a well-organised campaign of protest. It was reported that no fewer than 6,000 citizens attended one rally to voice their opposition to the resumption of transportation.

Despite the protests, some convicts were sent ashore at Sydney. The rest were taken on to Moreton Bay. The British Government decided not to send any more convicts to New South Wales, although it did continue to transport criminals to Tasmania until 1853.

Stirling had been adamant that the settlement he proposed for the Swan River should not be a destination for convicts. The Colonial Office endorsed that policy and issued a circular that stated *'It is not intended that any convicts or other description of Prisoners be sent to this new settlement.'*[20] In his *Manual for Emigrants,* published in 1839, Nathaniel Ogle claimed that:

> *Western Australia is happily without the taint of a penal colony. No convict has ever been landed there; and the great distance from the penal settlements renders it improbable that even any who have escaped into the bush could reach the confines of the district.*[21]

After stating that the colony was remarkably free of crime due to the lack of convicts, he added:

20 Colonial Office circular December 5 1828.
21 Ogle, p43.

'Even of the small number of offences committed against the laws, the greater proportion has originated among those who have come to this colony from the neighbouring penal settlements.'

In fact, there were convicts in Western Australia when settlers first arrived at the Swan River. Twenty three convicts had been brought to King George Sound on the *Amity* in 1826.

In the year that Ogle's *Manual for Immigrants* was published, the Colonial Office wrote to the Governor of Western Australia – John Hutt – asking if the colony would be prepared to accept some juvenile offenders who had been attending institutions where they had been educated and reformed. Hutt sought advice from the members of the Western Australian Agricultural Society before replying that the community would not object to boys under 15 years of age, but could not accept more than 30 boys each year. Over the next several years 234 boys were taken from Parkhurst Prison and sent out to Perth.

As the Swan River settlement struggled to survive, the idea of free convict labour began to appeal to some citizens. The members of the York Agricultural Society took up the campaign to have convicts brought to Western Australia as a solution to some of the Colony's problems. They passed a motion at one of their meetings in 1844 to petition 'the Secretary of State for the colonies for a gang of forty convicts to be exclusively employed on public works.'[22] The petition was ignored. The next year the Society delivered another petition, this time to the Colony's

22   JS Battye, *Western Australia – A History from its Discovery to the Inauguration of the Commonwealth*, Oxford University Press, 1924.

Legislative Council, asking that the Council approach the British Government and request that convicts be sent to the Swan River colony. In support of the petition the society claimed that the colony's economy was in serious trouble because of the shortage of labour. The council rejected the petition. It did not accept that there was a shortage of labour and considered the introduction of convicts to be a risky experiment.

Two years later the York Agricultural Society presented a third petition to the Legislative Council asking for transportation of convicts to Western Australia. This time the Council forwarded the petition to the Colonial Office and suggested the British Government might send out a small number of convicts for a limited term.[23]

Coincidentally, the British Government was at that time anxious to find a solution to prison overcrowding. Transportation to New South Wales had ceased in 1840 and the citizens of that colony were openly hostile to any resumption. In 1848 Charles Fitzgerald arrived in Perth to become Governor of Western Australia and he brought with him the Colonial Office's reply to the Legislative Council's suggestion. Transportation as a sentence would not be revived, the Colonial Office asserted, but the government would be agreeable to sending prisoners to Western Australia to serve out the final years of their sentences.

A public meeting was held in Perth to discuss the matter. The attendees realised that the Colonial Office's proposal meant that Western Australia would be receiving convicts but no financial support. They resolved to ask the British

23   P Statham, 'Why Convicts?', in CT Stannage (ed.), Convictism in Western Australia, University of Western Australia, 1981.

Government either to fund a convict establishment in Western Australia or not send out any convicts at all.

The British Government did not take long to decide that financing a convict establishment in Western Australians was the most convenient solution to overcrowded prisons. In 1850 the *Hashemy* set sail from Portland bound for the Swan River Colony. On board were 131 passengers and 100 convicts. That first one hundred was followed by thousands more. Almost 10,000 convicts from Britain served time in Western Australia. The Swan River Colony was the destination for British criminals sentenced to terms of transportation until 1868.

The people of Western Australia asked that no man convicted of a very serious crime, no female convicts and no political prisoners be transported to the colony. At first the British Government complied, but as soon as prisons suitable to house dangerous men had been constructed, some of the worst offenders were shipped out to Western Australia. No female convicts were transported, and it was not until the last load of convicts arrived on the *Hougoumont* that Western Australia received its first political prisoners: 62 members of the Irish Republican Brotherhood, commonly called 'Fenians'.

The first task of the convicts was to build their own accommodation. At Fremantle, convicts constructed the Convict Establishment and in Perth the Perth Gaol. When Western Australia ceased to be a destination for convicts, the British Government handed the Convict Establishment over to the Western Australian Government.

The Fremantle Prison – as it came to be known – served as the state's principal gaol until 1991.

The colony profited from the presence of the convicts. In Perth they built the Town Hall, with a broad arrow motif clearly evident in the stonework of the clock tower, and Government House. Not only did convicts provide a free labour force for the construction of public buildings and infrastructure, but they had to be fed with local produce supplied by Western Australian farmers and paid for by the British Government. Furthermore, they had to be guarded and so a substantial military force had to be based in the colony – again at the expense of the British Government. At the western end of Saint George's Terrace, an impressive Barracks was constructed to house soldiers and their families.

It was extremely difficult for convicts to escape from Western Australia. Men brought up in the towns of England were not likely to have the knowledge or skills to be able to survive in the Australian wilderness. The nearest outpost of civilization – South Australia – was some three thousand kilometres away and to get there a convict would have to trek through hundreds of kilometres of the waterless Nullarbor.

In 1841 the experienced explorer, Edward John Eyre, had set out to pioneer a route from South Australia to Albany. He had been well prepared with eleven pack horses, another explorer (Baxter) and three Australian aboriginal guides. After six months, he and one loyal companion – an aboriginal named Wyllie – reached Albany with practically nothing other than the ragged clothes they were wearing. That they had survived was probably due to the fact that near Esperance they had sighted a French whaling ship and the crew had looked after them, allowing them a few days of rest and replenishing their stores.[24]

One notorious convict – Joseph Bolitho Johns – did set out to escape to Adelaide, but he did not get very far. Johns arrived in Western Australia in 1853 to serve a ten-year sentence of penal servitude for theft. For a time he cooperated enough to earn a conditional release, and he went to live in the Avon Valley, in an area the aboriginals called Moondyne. He adopted 'Moondyne Joe' as his nickname.

It was not long before Moondyne Joe was in trouble with the law. He stole a horse and was arrested, broke free, stole the same horse and was recaptured and sentenced to serve three years as a prisoner. During the term of that sentence, he behaved so well that he was released with a ticket of leave.

While working on a farm at Kelmscott, Johns was arrested again. He was charged with stealing a neighbour's steer. Despite his protestations of innocence, he was found guilty and sentenced to ten years penal servitude. Again Johns managed to escape, and he survived for a time by robbing settlers, becoming Western Australia's only notorious bushranger.

It was not long before the police arrested him again. He was sentenced to serve twelve months in irons, but he somehow managed to cut off the irons and then embarked on a campaign of petty robbery with three other convicts. When one of his accomplices was caught, Johns realised that it would only be a matter of time before they all would be arrested as the police were making good use of aboriginal trackers. He and his small gang stole a supply of provisions and set off towards South Australia.

The explorer, Charles Cooke Hunt, had blazed a trail as far as where the town of Coolgardie was later established, and that trail Johns intended to follow. The bushrangers covered only about 300 kilometres before the police and aboriginal trackers caught up with them. Perhaps it was just as well that they were caught. Their chances of reaching South Australia would have been extremely slim. Johns and his followers had no experience of exploration and were not well equipped for such a long journey over some of the driest country on the planet.

Sentenced to a further five years of hard labour, Johns was given special attention by the prison authorities. Determined that he would not escape again, they had his cell at Fremantle made escape-proof by lining the stone walls with jarrah sleepers. Johns was made to perform hard labour – breaking up rocks – in a corner of the prison yard while being watched by a warder. The warders were not vigilant enough, for, behind his pile of rocks Johns aimed occasional blows at the wall until he had made a hole large enough to be able to escape yet again.

For two years Johns avoided capture by not attracting the attention of the constabulary until he made the mistake of attempting to steal wine from Houghton's Winery on a day when the police happened to be there. He never escaped again and he never did manage to get away from Western Australia. Johns ended his days in the Fremantle Lunatic Asylum suffering from senile dementia.

A few convicts did escape by sea, aided by crews of visiting ships. An Irish convict, John Boyle O'Reilly, who had arrived aboard the *Hougoumont* in 1868, was smuggled out of the colony on an American whaling ship. He settled in the United States where, with the help of some other Fenians, he planned to help his convict friends in Western Australia to escape. They purchased a three-masted whaler – the *Catalpa* – and sent her off on what was ostensibly a trading voyage. An advance party of two Irish republicans went to Western Australia to prepare for the rescue of the Fenian convicts, and they arranged for some men to be ready to cut the telegraph lines that had recently been erected connecting Fremantle to Perth.

On 17 April 1876 the *Catalpa*, anchored in international waters off the coast just south of Fremantle, sent a whaleboat to the beach to await the arrival of the escapees. Six Fenians absconded from a working party of convicts and hurried to where the whaleboat was waiting for them. They were seen, and the authorities were alerted. The escapees managed to board the *Catalpa* just before a steamship, with a large squad of officers on board, arrived.

Although the police boat had a cannon and over thirty armed men on board, no attempt was made to seize the *Catalpa* and recapture the convicts. The captain of the *Catalpa* raised the American Flag and claimed that any attempt to board his ship could be regarded as an act of war against the United States. Perhaps the prospect of provoking another war between America and Britain was an outcome the Western Australian authorities did not want to risk. The Anglo-American War (1812 – 1815) followed the boarding of a U.S. frigate by British sailors and the arrest of four British deserters. The police returned to Fremantle empty handed and the *Catalpa* made it back to New York without being intercepted by the Royal Navy.

The return of the *Catalpa* to New York was widely publicised and was celebrated in both the United States and Ireland by those who supported the campaign for Irish self-rule or those who disliked Great Britain. There is now a large memorial at Rockingham marking the site where, it is supposed, the six Fenians boarded the whaleboat and set off for the *Catalpa*.

Transportation to Western Australia ended with the arrival of the last transport ship, the *Hougoumont*, in January 1868, but there were thousands of convicts in Western Australia for years after that. It was not until every convict had either served out his sentence or died that Western Australia could claim once more to be 'happily without the taint of a penal colony.'

As the number of convicts in Western Australia dwindled, Britain withdrew its financial support. Buildings used in the convict system were handed over to the Colonial Government and officials, wardens and troops who had administered the system were withdrawn. The colony suffered a recession as a result. Frederick Weld, who was Governor of Western Australia from 1869 to 1875, wrote to the Secretary of State for the colonies protesting that Western Australia had first lost much by becoming a convict settlement, and had lost again by the cessation of transportation. He asserted that Western Australian colonies had not been adequately compensated, as they had suffered some particularly bad seasons and still had to support the *'criminals, lunatics and paupers'* that had been landed on its shores.

Chapter 8: *Gold!*

Losing the benefits of being a convict settlement would have affected Western Australia less had gold not been discovered in New South Wales and Victoria. Skilled immigrants were naturally inclined to settle in one of the colonies where it might be possible to strike gold, rather than the Swan River settlement with all its well-publicised problems.

Gold was first discovered in Australia at Fish River near Bathurst in New South Wales in 1823. Just a few flecks were found, though not enough to create a great deal of interest. Some twenty years later the Reverend W.B. Clarke found some nuggets in a creek near Lithgow. The Governor of New South Wales was reported to have told him, 'Put it away, Mister Clarke, or we shall all have our throats cut!' As a substantial part of the population of the colony consisted of convicted criminals, the governor had good reason to want news of the discovery to be suppressed.

In 1851 Edward Hargreaves found gold at Ophir near Bathurst, after transportation to New South Wales had ceased. News of the find spread rapidly. The result was the first Australian gold rush. Within a few months over a thousand men were at Ophir hoping to make their fortunes.

That same year Victoria was excised from New South Wales and granted the status of an independent colony. The authorities in Victoria, not wanting to lose any of their population to New South Wales, offered a reward to anyone finding gold within 200 kilometres of Melbourne. Just six months after the discovery at Ophir, far richer deposits of gold were found at Ballarat. People rushed to Ballarat, and later to Bendigo. The population of Victoria grew from 77,000 to 540,000 in just two years. For a time Melbourne was the major gateway to Australia and a larger city than Sydney.

In 1862, the Legislative Council of Western Australia, wanting the colony to enjoy the benefits of gold mining would bring, invited Edward Hargraves to come to the west and search for gold. Hargraves prospected without any success, and then declared that it was unlikely that gold would ever be found in the colony. In fact, a few small pieces of gold had been found near York in 1861.

In 1864 and 1865 Charles Cooke Hunt led working parties to clear a track eastward from York and to establish a series of wells to be used by pastoralists. This 'Old York Road' later came to be the route followed by diggers from Perth to the Goldfields. On a third expedition in 1866, he had with him four pensioner soldiers and three ticket-of-leave convicts. One of the convicts was an amateur geologist who spent much of his spare time looking for gold and he found a number of nuggets in a dry creek bed.

With the help of two other two convicts, they collected a sizeable amount of gold, stole horses and provisions, and set off for South Australia. After realising that they were not likely to reach Adelaide, and it would be better to be captured than to die in the desert, they returned to surrender themselves to Hunt.

Hunt did not publicise the convicts' discovery of gold, but word leaked out and many prospectors set out to find the 'Convict's Gold'. None had any success until 1888 when Giles McPherson found some nuggets near where, he assumed, the convicts had found theirs. In 1892 Jack Reidy also claimed to have found the Convicts' Gold. Reidy's Hill near Coolgardie did yield a considerable amount of alluvial gold.

With financial support from the British Government for the convict system being wound back, the Western Australian Government badly needed the economic boost gold mines would provide. In 1872, it offered a reward of five thousand pounds to anyone who found a profitable gold deposit. The reward was never paid due to the strict conditions; the find had to be within 180 kilometres of a port and produce 10,000 ounces of gold in two years.

In 1882, prospectors recovered alluvial gold from the upper reaches of the Ord River in the far north of the colony. A geologist – Edward Harman – was sent to investigate the find and he succeeded in panning gold from a number of creeks in the Kimberley. A group of prospectors led by Charles Hall found worthwhile amounts of the precious metal in what became known as Halls Creek. Men rushed to Hall's Creek and a town developed that, at the peak of the gold rush, had a population that had been estimated at anywhere from two to eight thousand. The supply of easily obtainable gold was soon exhausted and within a few years the population of Hall's Creek had dwindled to just a few hundred.

Encouraged by the find at Hall's Creek, prospectors looked for gold elsewhere and it was not long before gold was found in the Pilbara. Marble Bar became the centre for gold mining in the area and by 1887 the town had a population of over 5,000. Several particularly large nuggets were found at Marble Bar, the largest of which – called the Bobby Dazzler – weighed 413 ounces.

Further south, gold was found in the area that later became the town of Southern Cross. The prospectors who made the find – Thomas Riseley and Mick Toomey – claimed that it was the Southern Cross constellation that guided them to the gold. Within a few years, far richer deposits had been found at Coolgardie; Southern Cross became a centre for pastoralists and a staging post on the route from Perth to the east. Southern Cross was the site of the first mine in Western Australia to be owned by an incorporated company that paid dividends to shareholders.

In 1892 Arthur Wellesley Bayley sparked the greatest gold rush in the history of Western Australia when he arrived in Southern Cross with 554 ounces of gold that he had found at Fly Flat, near Coolgardie. Within a decade Kalgoorlie had been established as the main centre of the Goldfields. The town's population had grown to some 30,000 people, and boasted no less than 93 hotels and 8 breweries.

Among those who came to Western Australia to make their fortunes by finding gold were diggers from Victoria and New South Wales – where all the easy finds had been exhausted – and Americans from the Californian goldfields. The most celebrated miners to strike gold were three Irishmen: Paddy Hannan, Tom Flanagan and Daniel Shea.

Hannan, Flanagan and Shea were a part of a large group of prospectors who, in 1893, intended to try their luck at Mount Yule, east of Coolgardie. While they were camped at Mount Charlotte waiting for supplies of water and food to arrive, Hannan found some gold nuggets in a gully. He and his two friends then took their horse into the bush and left it there. When the other prospectors moved on the next day, the three Irishmen claimed their horse had strayed and they had to stay to find it. After the rest of the prospectors had left, the three gathered all the gold they could find and pegged out a claim. Hannan, the only one of the three who was literate, went into Coolgardie and registered their claim.

News of the three Irishmen's good fortune spread rapidly and their pegged-out lot was soon surrounded by other claims. However, it was not their claimed area that proved to be the main source of gold near Kalgoorlie. Within a few years, disappointed miners were moving on to look elsewhere. It was just south of Kalgoorlie that prospectors discovered the deep reefs of the Boulder Fault that came to be known as the Golden Mile. The town of Boulder grew beside the Golden Mile and spread until it became joined to Kalgoorlie in one sprawling city.

Kalgoorlie-Boulder, as it is called, now claims to be Australia's largest outback city.

News that some of the richest deposits of gold in the world had been discovered in Western Australia caused investors in Britain to look for opportunities to become involved. In 1896, a rich body of ore was found some 320 kilometres north of Kalgoorlie and George W. Hall purchased the mining rights from the prospectors who had made the find. Seeking capital to enable him to make the most from his investment, Hall contacted financiers in London. The financing company employed a 23 year old American mining engineer named Herbert Hoover to assess the potential of the mine. Hoover was impressed and asked to be appointed to manage the project. A syndicate called Sons of Gwalia[25] was formed to finance the project. Hoover ensured it enjoyed a healthy profit by bringing in Italian immigrants who were hard workers, comparatively cheap to hire and uninvolved in the Trade Union Movement. He went on to work at other Western Australian mines – Big Bell, Cue, Leonora, Menzies and Coolgardie – before returning to America where he was elected President (1929-1933).

A small town near the Gwalia mine housed some workers, but the principal town for the area was – and is – Leonora, just a few kilometres away. Leonora was linked to Kalgoorlie by rail in 1902 and continues to be a centre for gold and nickel mining while Gwalia became almost a ghost town.

As most of the easily-recovered gold in Western Australia was removed by prospectors, miners had to dig

25 "Gwalia" is an ancient name for Wales. It was a syndicate of Welshmen who financed the development of the mine.

deeper and work harder to extract small amounts of the precious metal from large quantities of ore. Gold mining became the province of companies that had substantial capital and could invest in expensive machinery. Dozens of public and proprietary companies were incorporated to mine Western Australia's gold. The state became the beneficiary of an inflow of a considerable amount of capital and technology.

Although almost all of the easily-recoverable gold has been mined and the days of individual prospectors digging and panning and striking it rich are over – unless one is extraordinarily lucky – gold mining remains one of the State's major industries.

The benefits that flowed to Western Australia from the discovery of gold were far greater than just the economic boost that gold provided.

Geology became a popular choice as an occupation for young men and the study of geology became a popular course at the University of Western Australia. Geologists and prospectors found not only gold but a wide range of other minerals.

The population of the state was suddenly and significantly increased by the influx of miners and their families. According to the Western Australian Genealogical Society about 26,000 people arrived in the colony in the fifty years between 1839 and 1890, including all convicts, their guards and others involved in the convict system. In the thirty years after 1898 over 430,000 people arrived. No doubt there would have been a considerable boost to the population of the colony in years of the initial gold rushes.

One important legacy of the development of the mines at Kalgoorlie, Boulder and Coolgardie is the Mundaring to Kalgoorlie pipeline. Much of the credit for that must be accorded to C.Y. O'Connor.

Charles Yelverton O'Connor was born in County Meath, Ireland, in 1843. At the age of 21, he migrated to New Zealand where he rose to being the Marine Engineer for the country. In 1891, he accepted the position of Engineer in Chief in Western Australia. His first major project was to establish a harbour at the mouth of the Swan River. Disregarding critics who claimed that he would not be successful because the harbour would soon silt up, O'Connor had the limestone bar and the accumulated sand removed from the Swan River estuary, then had moles constructed north and south of the mouth of the river. In 1897, a passenger liner from England entered the harbour O'Connor had formed, and for the first time a large ocean-going ship was able to be berthed at Victoria Quay at Fremantle – named in honour of Queen Victoria.

O'Connor next set to work to ensure that the Goldfields had a reliable supply of fresh water. Despite criticism in the local press and from members of the West Australian parliament, O'Connor persevered on construction of a pipeline from Mundaring Weir, in the hills behind Perth, to a reservoir at Kalgoorlie. That meant a pipeline about 530 kilometres long with pumping stations at various intervals to push the water up to the plateau on which Kalgoorlie had been built.

Less than a year before the first water was pumped into the reservoir at Mount Charlotte, O'Connor committed suicide by shooting himself on 10 March 1902. Perhaps an article in the Sunday Times a few weeks previously had made him decide to take his own life.

That article contained this libellous passage:

> *Apart from any distinct charge of corruption this man had exhibited such gross blundering or something worse in his management of great public works it is no great exaggeration to say that he has robbed the taxpayer of this state of many millions of money... This crocodile has been backed up in all his reckless extravagant juggling with public funds, in all his nefarious machinations behind the scenes by the kindred-souled editor of the West Australian.*[26]

An investigation by the Western Australian Government cleared O'Connor of any charges of corruption or of any misdemeanours in the discharge of his duties. He is now recognised as one of the most important men in the history of Western Australia.

The pipeline that O'Connor established not only supplies water to Kalgoorlie-Boulder, but also provides a reliable supply of water to towns and farms along its route.

26   AG Evans, *C.Y. O'Connor, his Life and Legacy*, University of Western Australia Press, 2001.

Chapter 9: *Other Natural Assets*

The Dutch explorer, Jan Carstenz, was mistaken when he dismissed New Holland as a land where there was not *'anything that man may make use of'.*[27] Western Australia contains vast areas that settlers found suitable for agriculture, other areas ideal for pastoral activities and arguably the richest goldfields in the world. Nature had bestowed upon the state an abundance of other resources that man could made use of.

SEALS

Australia's first exports were seal skins and oil extracted from the carcases. In 1798 hunters from Sydney went to islands in Bass Strait and slaughtered dozens of seals. It was easy work and seal skins and oil found a ready market in Britain.

From Bass Strait the sealers moved westward and discovered small islands off the south coast of Western Australia where seals were to be found in abundance. Before the first official settlement was established at King George Sound in 1826 sealers were already living on the nearby islands.

---

27 For more of Carstenz' comments see Chapter 2

So efficient were the sealers that by 1830 the number of seals had been so reduced that the British Government feared they would become extinct. Seal Hunting was made illegal. Since then the number of seals visiting the coast of Western Australia has recovered to a large extent recovered.

WHALES

Settlers hunted whales for oil and bone. When Western Australia was first settled, sightings of whales were almost an every-day occurrence, but hunting them was far more difficult than hunting seals. Hunters in rowing boats would have to pursue their prey until it surfaced close enough to be speared with a harpoon hurled by a man with a strong arm. It might take a long time for the whale to die, and then it would have to be towed back to the shore or to a ship. Hunting that way would not have drastically reduced the whale population. It was the later use of explosive harpoons fired from cannons, faster and larger ships that depleted the stock of whales almost to the point of extinction and provoked international action to save the species.

Whaling in Western Australia became a large-scale commercial enterprise in 1873 when two whaling companies – the Fremantle Whaling Company and the Perth Whaling Company – commenced operations. The Perth Whaling Company established its base on Carnac Island while the Fremantle Company operated from the beach near Fremantle. So successful was the Fremantle Whaling Company that the government had a tunnel cut through the hill that stands between the town of

Fremantle and the beach to allow easier distribution of the company's products. In their first year of operation the two whaling companies generated more revenue than the Colony's graziers did from the sale of wool.

In addition to those two companies, there were other corporations and individuals that sought to profit from killing whales. The Castle Rock Whaling company was based at Dunsborough, and the Bussell family was for a time involved in whaling from Augusta. Thomas Peel also considered whaling as a solution to his financial problems. He came across some aboriginal men eating the meat of a beached whale near Safety Bay, and he enlisted their help to build a fire and extract oil from the blubber. He then attempted to obtain the backing to set up a whaling business, but nobody was prepared to finance him.

The local whaling companies faced serious competition from American and French whalers. 'Yankee' Whalers were even known to pursue their prey into Cockburn Sound. The Legislative Council passed a law prohibiting unlicensed whalers from hunting in Western Australian waters, but that was difficult to enforce and was largely ignored.

It was probably the development of petroleum products for lubrication and heating that saved the whales from being hunted to extinction. The way to refine crude oil was discovered around the mid-nineteenth century, and then kerosene, a fuel far superior to oil from animals became available. As the world's production of petroleum increased the demand and the price of whale oil declined. By the turn of the century, the number of whale hunters had been significantly reduced.

The killing of whales for meat and oil continued. In 1912, the Western Australian Government gave a Norwegian whaling company permission to establish bases at Albany and Point Cloates at North West Cape. Using exploding harpoons fired out of cannons on fast chaser boats, the Norwegians had a few profitable years, but the resultant decline in whale numbers led to the closure of the company's Western Australian base in 1916. The facilities at Point Cloates remained unused until the 1930's when the Norwegians serviced their ships there.

Albany became a major centre for whaling in Western Australia after the Second World War. The Albany Whaling Company was established in 1947, but it could not kill enough whales to be viable and was closed after just three years. The Cheynes Beach Whaling Company, based at Frenchman's Bay, began hunting whales in 1952. It was more successful, but pressure from environmentalists contributed to the decision to cease operations in 1978.

In 1949 the Nor'-West Whaling Company began operating out of Point Cloates, and the next year the Australian Whaling Commission – a Commonwealth Government enterprise – commenced operations from Babbage Island near Carnarvon. The government whalers were said to have harvested about 600 whales each year and to have made a satisfactory profit, but after about ten years of being involved in whaling the government decided that it was not politically advisable to be slaughtering whales while so many electors were campaigning against whaling. The Babbage Island site was sold to Nor'-West Whaling. It changed its name to Nor'-West Seafoods and now uses the old whaling station to process seafoods other than whale meat. It also conducts whale-watching tours.

SALT

In the early days of the Western Australia colony, salt was valued not only as an essential dietary supplement, but also for its ability to preserve meats. Salted meats were an important part of the rations on every ship. When explorers went to the Murchison River in the 1850s to mine lead, they were pleased to find substantial deposits of salt which were collected and shipped to Britain along with the lead.

With the development of chemical industries, salt became even more sought after as a source of sodium, chlorine, magnesium, potassium, iodine and bromine. Australia is now one of the world's major producers of salt, and most Australian salt comes from Western Australia.

GUANO

The Europeans method of fertilisation – digging manure from domestic animals through the soil – came with the settlers.

Off the coast of Western Australia are islands rich with deposits of seals and sea birds droppings. By 1850 colonists had discovered that the Abrolhos Islands carried tons of seal guano and the Lacepede Islands off Shark Bay had a thick layer of bird guano. Entrepreneurs gathered as much as possible to sell on the mainland, or export to Britain.

So much fertilizer was taken to Britain that the export of guano came to be second only to wool as the top export for the colony. The Legislative Council decided to control the exploitation of the guano deposits, and to collect royalties. The royalty was set at 2 pounds per ton, but there were complaints to the Colonial Office that the charge was exorbitant. The Colonial Office stepped in and halved the rate, but Guano harvesters easily avoided paying any royalty at all because the colony just did not have the resources to police all those scattered, remote islands. In 1876, a Victorian syndicate by the name of Poole, Picken and Company offered to pay a royalty of just 10 shillings per ton if granted an exclusive licence to harvest the guano from the Lacepedes. The offer was accepted by the Western Australian authorities.

William Roberts, an American who visited the Lacepede Islands, recognised the potential money to be made from the guano there, and went to Melbourne to consult the American Vice-Consul-General – Samuel Perkins Lord. Lord decided that the islands, 30 kilometres off the coast, were outside the territorial waters of the Colony of Western Australia. He declared them to be possessions of the United States of America and authorised Roberts to go there and harvest the guano.

Roberts chartered a French ship and set sail for the Lacepedes. When he arrived, he found employees of Poole, Picken and Company loading guano onto two ships. There was a heated argument, and one of the men from Poole, Picken and Company sailed to Roebourne to get support. He obtained a warrant to seize the French ship.

The French ship was fully loaded when the man sent to Roebourne arrived back at the Lacepede islands.

The French skipper did not dispute the validity of the warrant and agreed to sail to Roebourne. There was a trial and Roberts was fined £100. The French skipper paid the prescribed 10 shillings per ton royalty, and left for Europe with a full cargo of guano.

The Governor of Western Australia, William Robinson, informed the Colonial Office of what Lord had done, and the British Government sent a protest to Washington. The president of the United States, Ulysses S. Grant, obligingly repudiated Lord's 'annexation' of the Western Australian islands.

The supply of guano was rapidly depleted. In 1879 the Colonial Government called for tenders to collect what was left, claiming that there was no less than 40,000 tons. A British firm, McDonald and Mockford, had its tender accepted, but when its men went to the islands they found that only about 15,000 tons of guano remained and that was of poor quality. The Colonial Government agreed to pay McDonald and Mockford 9,783 pounds in damages.[28]

Guano mining on the Lacepedes ceased completely in the 1880s. In 1970 the islands were made a nature reserve.

The Abrolhos Island continued to be a source of guano until 1904. The Western Australian Government then forbade the further exportation of guano. The islands are now an A class reserve managed by the Department of Fisheries for the conservation of flora and fauna, for tourism and for the fishing industry.

Superphosphate – a fertiliser created from sulphuric acid and powdered phosphate rock – replaced guano in 1910 and the demand for guano tapered away after that.

28 See the Kimberley Society website at www.kimberleysociety.org/oldfiles.

PEARLS

When Francis Gregory returned to Perth in 1861 after exploring the Champion Bay district, he brought not only news that the land was arable, but also some pearl shell and a good pearl that the crew of his ship, the *Dolphin*, had collected in what became known as Nickol Bay. Soon not only pastoralists but also men hoping to make a fortune from pearling were arriving at the port of Cossack.

The pearling industry based at Cossack was not the first such enterprise in Western Australia. Indigenous Australians had, for centuries, collected pearl shell and used it for decorative purposes. There is evidence that whale hunters visiting the coast in the 1840s had also collected shells. An American whaling ship, the *Cervantes*, which was wrecked in 1844 near where the town that bears its name now stands, was carrying pearl shell.[29] British settlers had collected shell and pearls in Shark Bay in the 1850s, but that venture lasted for just a few years.

Some of the more notable characters in the colony who became involved in the business of pearling out of Cossack included: the pioneer pastoralist, John Withnell the merchant and philanthropist, Walter Padbury; the pastoralist and member of the Legislative Council, Charles Broadhurst; and Charles Harper who was a pastoralist, a member of the Legislative Council and one of the proprietors of the *West Australian* newspaper.

At first the pearl fishers collected the shells that could be reached while wading at low tide, but the supplies of shell in the shallows were soon depleted. When it became

---

29   M McCarthy, 'Naked Diving for Mother of Pearl', *Early Days – Journals and Proceedings of the Royal Western Australian Historical Society*, vol. 13, Part 2, p243.

necessary to dive in deeper waters, Cossack was abandoned by the pearl fishers who moved to Broome.

Australian aboriginals were often employed to do the diving, and later 'Malays' (Indonesians) were brought in to do what was a difficult and dangerous task. Some divers were taken by sharks and many were drowned in the cyclones that strike the North West from time to time. Towards the end of the nineteenth century the development of diving suits with air supplied by pumps made it possible for divers to work at greater depths and to spend more time gathering the shells. However, upon returning to the surface divers were likely to suffer from the bends, which could cause serious permanent injury, even paralysis or death. They were generally poorly paid for the hazardous work. The exact number of those who died while attempting to retrieve pearl shell is not known, but in the years between 1908 and 1935 alone more than 100 pearling boats were wrecked by the storms and more than 300 men perished.[30]

In the first half of the next century, Broome was the most important pearling centre in the world. By 1910 nearly 400 luggers were working out of its port and the industry was employing over 3,500 people.[31]

The development of plastics destroyed the market for pearl shell after the First World War. Most pearl shell had been used to make buttons and buckles which are easy to mass produce from a newly-invented material: plastics. Pearling became primarily a search for pearls, but it was a dying industry. By 1939 only 565 people in Western Australia were still trying to earn money from pearling,

30 See 'The History of Pearling in Western Australia', at the Western Australian Department of Fisheries website at www.fish.wa.gov.au.
31 *Ibid*

and the end of the Second World War there were only 15 boats and about 200 people working in the pearling industry out of Broome. Pearlers turned to artificially creating pearls instead.

In 1922, the Australian Government, in an attempt to save the pearl fishing industry, passed an act forbidding the artificial production of pearls. The act was repealed in 1949 and Australians in the pearling industry looked to Japan. The Japanese had discovered how to make an oyster produce first-grade pearls. There are now five pearl farms in Western Australia. Western Australia, with Japanese help, is producing much of the world's supply of cultivated pearls.

DIAMONDS

Some diamonds were found in the Pilbara in the 1890's, but there were not of a high enough quality or quantity to motivate anyone to search for the source of the gems. It was not until 1972 that geologists became convinced that there could be worthwhile deposits of diamonds in the Kimberley area. Some five years later a number of diamond-bearing pipes were found near Derby, but they proved to be uneconomic. In 1979 geologists discovered what has been claimed to be the richest diamond deposit in the world – the Argyle Diamond Pipe near Lake Argyle.

In the 1960s the Western Australian and Commonwealth Governments had decided to dam the Ord River. It was thought that an irrigated area below the dam could become a major producer of food and could encourage the growth of the population in the area. The dam created the second largest artificial lake in Australia – Lake Argyle – but attempts to use its water to grow crops had disappointing results. The town established nearby – Kununurra – attracted few settlers.

The discovery of diamonds near Lake Argyle has justified the expense of constructing the dam on the Ord River. The Argyle mine is now the world's greatest producer of diamonds. About half of the diamonds are of industrial quality, and about 5 per cent are high quality gems including the rare pink, champagne and cognac colours.

In 1984, Argyle Diamonds set up a diamond polishing business in Perth, effectively breaking the control of the diamond industry that the South African company, De Beers, had exercised since the end of the nineteenth century.

COAL

Western Australia does not contain rich deposits of coal like those in New South Wales and Queensland – or, at least, none have yet been discovered – but it does have enough coal to be self-sufficient.

The nineteenth century was an age of steam power. In 1839, hoping to further the interests of the struggling colony, the Western Australian Government offered a reward of 2,560 acres of land to anyone who found a commercial coalfield south of Shark Bay. It was never claimed.

Some coal was found near the Murray River in 1846 and this led to the formation of the Western Australian Mining Company. Bore sinking was undertaken, but produced disappointing results and the company closed.

Coal was then discovered in 1846 near the Irwin River by Augustus Gregory, but it was deemed uneconomical to mine and transport to Perth. There was plenty of wood to burn in the Swan Valley, and coal could be imported from New South Wales if it was needed.

In 1883, George Marsh and Arthur Perrin found a rich seam of coal on the banks of the Collie River. Exploitation of the find took several years to begin and it was not until 1889 that the first coal was recovered from shallow shafts.

In 1893, C.Y. O'Connor, the Colony's Engineer in Chief, began to urge the government to take steps to make Western Australia self-sufficient in terms of coal. By that time, steam-powered ships were making sailing ships obsolete and there was an obvious market for coal to re-fuel ships calling in at Fremantle.

A government mine at Collie was established in 1896, and two years later the Colony's first underground mine began production. The Collie Coalfield is still Western Australia's only coal mine. Coal from it has been the fuel for the State's main electrical power generators for years. There are currently seven mines at Collie – three underground and four open cut.

Exploration for petroleum and other minerals subsequently revealed the existence of a number of other coal seams in the state, but as yet none of those has been exploited.

ASBESTOS

Asbestos was once valued in the industrial world for its fire-resistance, its insulating qualities, and its use as a binding element in the manufacture of fibro-cement panels.

In 1917, the Western Australian Mines Department recorded the discovery of asbestos in the state, but it was not until 1937 that anyone began to mine. The man responsible for the first asbestos mine was Lang Hancock. He was interested in geology, and while exploring the gorges of the Hamersley Ranges in 1919, while still a young boy, he found blue asbestos. In 1934 he staked a claim for an asbestos mine, and four years later he began collecting the asbestos and transporting it by horseback to Point Samson for export.

The Second World War created a boom market for asbestos. Because of its absolute resistance to fire, it was widely used in machines of war. Hancock sold a 51 per cent share in his mine to Australian Blue Asbestos Pty Ltd. A town named Wittenoom was built to house workers. From 1950 to 1960, Wittenoom Gorge provided all the asbestos used in Australia and a considerable amount for export.

In 1948, Dr Eric Saint warned the Western Australian Department of Health that workers and their families at Wittenoom would suffer from asbestosis. They were working every day in clouds of asbestos dust and the streets of Wittenoom were constructed with the tailings from the mine. Dr Saint's warnings were not taken seriously, and it was not until 1966 that Australian Blue Asbestos decided to close down its mine.

Even though the mine was closed and the threat to health that asbestos posed had been publicised, people continued to live at Wittenoom and tourists went there to explore the gorges and the mine. It was many years before the Western Australian Government took action as a result of Dr Saint's report. In 1978 it decided to close down the town of Wittenoom. Government services were gradually withdrawn and residents were offered help to relocate. Some refused to leave; closing down the town was a slow process. It was not until 2006 that the government withdrew its last measure of support for the town by turning off the supply of electricity. Two years later the town was declared to be a contaminated site.

About seven thousand people were employed by Australian Blue Asbestos between 1943 and 1966. It has been calculated that about 700 of them would have developed the fatal condition called mesothelioma. CSR Limited's annual report for the financial year ending in 2010 stated it had made provision for liability to the amount of $455.3 million.

URANIUM

Uranium is another dangerous natural asset found in Western Australia. With the development of nuclear science during the Second World War, uranium, which had been little more than a scientific curiosity, suddenly became a highly sought-after mineral. Not only could it be used to create powerful weapons, it could also generate electricity without producing any greenhouse gases, allowing ships and submarines to travel thousands of kilometres without refuelling.

Mines in South Australia and the Northern Territory were developed to capitalize on the demand for uranium. Deposits of the ore were located in Western Australia at Yeelirrie, Wiluna and Lake Maitland, but the establishment of mines was a subject of heated debate. Environmentalists argued that uranium is so dangerous that it should be left in the ground. The incredible power of atomic bombs and the terrible consequences of exposure to atomic radiation had been demonstrated in the bombing of Hiroshima and Nagasaki, and the serious consequences of trouble at a nuclear power station were made tragically clear by the accident at Chernobyl in 1986. The Yeelirrie deposit was discovered by the Western Mining Corporation in 1972, but it was not allowed to do anything to exploit its discovery until an Environment Impact Statement had been prepared. The study was completed by January 1979 and work was allowed to begin to prepare for open-cut mining. A pilot processing plant was built at Kalgoorlie and some ore was taken from three shallow slots. About $35 million dollars was spent by Western Mining in preparing for production, then the Labor Party won the 1983 Federal election and adopted a 'Three Mines' policy regarding uranium. The mines in South Australia and the Northern Territory were allowed to continue to operate, but work at Yeelirrie was forced to cease. The State Labor Government elected in Western Australia in 2002 revoked the mining agreement regarding Yeelirrie and demanded the restoration of the environment. The slots from which ore had been extracted were filled in and the site restored to its natural state.

In November, 2008, a newly elected State Liberal/ Country Party Government announced that it would lift the ban on uranium mining. Anticipating that would happen, the Canadian mining company Cameco and Japan's Mitsubishi agreed to buy from Rio Tinto the mining rights over a vast body of uranium in the Pilbara at Kintyre. At the time of writing this account (late 2011) there were no uranium mines in production in Western Australia, but four were the subject of feasibility studies. In addition to Kintyre, work had begun again at Yeelirrie and other mine sites were being assessed near Wiluna and Lake Maitland.

LEAD

Lead is yet another of Western Australia's natural assets that has proved to be a mixed blessing.

Since ancient times lead has been valued highly by civilised man. It melts at a comparatively low temperature, is soft enough to be hammered into a desired shape and is corrosion-resistant and, easily joined by the application of heat. The state's first venture into lead mining was, as mentioned in Chapter 9, the Geraldine lead mine at the Murchison River in the 1850s. Lead ore was subsequently discovered and mined at nearby Northampton.

The search for gold resulted in the discovery of other deposits of lead. At Whim Creek in the Pilbara, for example, the gold mine produced not only gold but also some silver, copper, zinc and lead.

In the nineteenth century scie
Robert Koch, the founder of modern
realised that lead is a persistent,
Despite that, the demand for lead is
Modern technology requires the use of lea
an effective shield against radiation, is the s
electronics and is the basis of most batteries.

In 2007, bulk lead carbonate from the Magell
was being exported through the Port of Espe
Investigations revealed that many children in the to
had seriously high levels of lead in their bodies. Th
State Government ordered Magellan to cease its mining
activities while a safer way of exporting the lead was
devised. In the meanwhile, no more bulk lead was to be
sent to Esperance. Magellan was also ordered to clean up
every trace of lead carbonate. The export of lead has been
resumed through the port of Fremantle.

Minerals and Metals Group struck similar trouble
with pollution at the port of Geraldton. Lead had been
extracted from the Golden Grove deposit about 280
kilometres to the east and shipped out of Geraldton for
some twenty years before, in December 2010, a serious
level of lead contamination was detected at the port.
The Government ordered MMG to cease sending lead
to Geraldton. The company cleaned up its facilities and
introduced safer methods for transporting the metal.
Permission to resume exporting through the port was
granted in October 2011. Since the mine employs almost
500 workers, its operations are important to the nearby
isolated small town of Yalgoo.

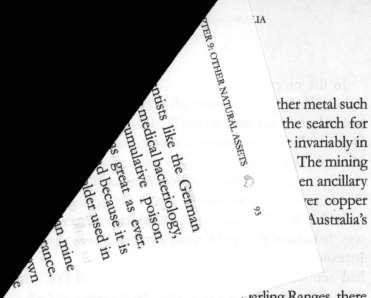

ther metal such
the search for
t invariably in
The mining
en ancillary
ver copper
Australia's

...Darling Ranges, there
... – hydrated aluminium oxide.

... cost-effective way of producing pure
...um from bauxite was first devised in 1886. The world's total production of aluminium in 1886 was just 45 kilograms. By 1990 world production of aluminium had risen to over 18 million tonnes per annum.

Alcoa, the world's leading producer of primary and fabricated aluminium, began mining bauxite at Jarrahdale in 1963. The bauxite was taken by rail to a refinery at Kwinana. During the 35 years that the Jarrahdale mine was operational, 160 million tons of bauxite was extracted, and then – to satisfy environmentalists – the area was carefully rehabilitated.

In 1972 Alcoa opened a second bauxite mine not far from Pinjarra. It established a new refinery at Pinjarra and constructed a long conveyor belt to carry the ore from the mine to the refinery. That mine was operational for about 20 years and extracted over 54 million tonnes

In the nineteenth century scientists like the German Robert Koch, the founder of modern medical bacteriology, realised that lead is a persistent, cumulative poison. Despite that, the demand for lead is as great as ever. Modern technology requires the use of lead because it is an effective shield against radiation, is the solder used in electronics and is the basis of most batteries.

In 2007, bulk lead carbonate from the Magellan mine was being exported through the Port of Esperance. Investigations revealed that many children in the town had seriously high levels of lead in their bodies. The State Government ordered Magellan to cease its mining activities while a safer way of exporting the lead was devised. In the meanwhile, no more bulk lead was to be sent to Esperance. Magellan was also ordered to clean up every trace of lead carbonate. The export of lead has been resumed through the port of Fremantle.

Minerals and Metals Group struck similar trouble with pollution at the port of Geraldton. Lead had been extracted from the Golden Grove deposit about 280 kilometres to the east and shipped out of Geraldton for some twenty years before, in December 2010, a serious level of lead contamination was detected at the port. The Government ordered MMG to cease sending lead to Geraldton. The company cleaned up its facilities and introduced safer methods for transporting the metal. Permission to resume exporting through the port was granted in October 2011. Since the mine employs almost 500 workers, its operations are important to the nearby isolated small town of Yalgoo.

COPPER

Copper is usually found in the presence of other metal such as gold, silver or lead. In Western Australia the search for gold revealed some deposits of copper, almost invariably in the form of azurite – also called blue malachite. The mining of copper in Western Australia has only ever been ancillary to gold mining. No mines specifically to recover copper have ever been established. Only about 7% of Australia's copper production comes from Western Australia.

BAUXITE

In the hills behind Perth, known as the Darling Ranges, there are vast deposits of bauxite – hydrated aluminium oxide.

A practical, cost-effective way of producing pure aluminium from bauxite was first devised in 1886. The world's total production of aluminium in 1886 was just 45 kilograms. By 1990 world production of aluminium had risen to over 18 million tonnes per annum.

Alcoa, the world's leading producer of primary and fabricated aluminium, began mining bauxite at Jarrahdale in 1963. The bauxite was taken by rail to a refinery at Kwinana. During the 35 years that the Jarrahdale mine was operational, 160 million tons of bauxite was extracted, and then – to satisfy environmentalists – the area was carefully rehabilitated.

In 1972 Alcoa opened a second bauxite mine not far from Pinjarra. It established a new refinery at Pinjarra and constructed a long conveyor belt to carry the ore from the mine to the refinery. That mine was operational for about 20 years and extracted over 54 million tonnes of ore. Again, the company was at pains to restore the ecosystem.

Such is the world's demand for aluminium that Alcoa subsequently established two more mines, Huntly and Willowdale, and a new refinery at Wagerup. Huntley has become the world's largest bauxite mine. Western Australia has become a major producer of aluminium for the world, and the mining and refining of aluminium have become important to the economy of the state.

NICKEL AND COBALT

Almost all of Australia's nickel production comes from Western Australia. The state supplies about 13% of the world's demand for the metal, which is an important element in various alloys – notably, stainless steel – and in nickel hydride batteries.

Cobalt is found in laterite nickel ore and is actually more valuable than the nickel. It is used in making the superalloys needed for jet engines and hard tools, and is also an element in some batteries.

Nickel ore was first discovered in Western Australia about 30 kilometres south of Kalgoorlie, in 1954. Western Mining Corporation constructed a new town, Kambalda, to house its workers and began mining the ore in 1966. The Vietnam War caused the price of nickel to rise and the value of shares in Western Mining Corporation increased considerably.

In 1969 the workers at Inco's mine in Canada – a major supplier of nickel to the world's markets – went out on strike. The price of nickel reached new heights. A Western Australian company, Poseidon NL - the shares in which were trading at just 80 cents each at the time – announced that it had found deposits of nickel ore at Windarra near Laverton. Investors rushed to buy shares in Poseidon. Within a few weeks the shares were being sold for over $12 each. By January 1970 investors were paying $280 for just one Poseidon share. It seemed to many people that a fortune could be made from investing in shares in mining companies. Shares in small mining companies were purchased for unjustifiably high prices.

The notorious 'Poseidon bubble' was destined to burst. The strike in Canada ended and the price of nickel fell. Poseidon began mining and found that its ore was of a lower grade than it had expected. The company became insolvent and was delisted in 1976.

Western Mining Corporation, by contrast, enjoyed sustained growth through its concentration on nickel. It established two open-cut mines north of Kalgoorlie – at Leinster and at Mount Keith – and built a smelter 15 kilometres south of Kalgoorlie to treat the ore from its three mines in the area. The smelter produces nickel matte, which is then shipped to the company's refinery at Kwinana and produces about 67,000 tonnes of nickel annually.[32]

There are a number of other companies involved in mining nickel in Western Australia – at Ravensthorpe, Cawse, Murrin Murrin and Bulong.

Murrin Murrin, situated just east of Leonora, is a particularly ambitious project. Operated by Anaconda Nickel and Glencore International, the capital cost has been quoted at one billion dollars.[33] With almost 1,000

32 www.australianmineatlas.gov.au/education/fact_sheets/nickel. Retrieved 24/01/2011
33 www.chemlink.com.au/nickel. Retrieved 24/01/2011

employees and contractors working at the mine, it is one of the largest single-site employers in the State. In 2009 the mine yielded 32,977 tonnes of nickel and 2,350 tonnes of cobalt.[34]

TIN AND TANTALUM

The existence of tin in Western Australia at Greenbushes, not far inland from Bunbury, was noted in a government geological survey in 1886. Mining the metal began two years later and is still carried out today. Tin was highly valued in the early days of the Colony as an essential element in bronze and for coating steel plate to make 'tin cans'. Most of Australia's tin comes from Tasmania, but the Greenbushes mine remains the country's second most important source of the metal and is one of the oldest tin mines in Australia.

The presence of tantalum in the Greenbushes mine was known as early as 1893, but then it had no use and was regarded as a nuisance. It first came to be valued when its extremely high melting point was recognised and it was used in the filaments of electric light globes. Tantalum was recently found to have twice the capacitance of any other known substance and it became an important element in electronics. The production of tantalum is now just as important as the mining of tin for the Greenbushes mine.

LITHIUM

In 1949 some ore from the Greenbushes mine was found to contain spodumene – the ore from which lithium can be refined. Further drilling revealed that Greenbushes has what is reputed to be the richest body of spodumene ever discovered.

Lithium was used in the nineteenth century to treat gout. It was also found to be a useful mood stabiliser and came to be the standard treatment for bi-polar disorder. In recent times it has come to be used in making lubricants for high-temperature applications and in the manufacture of ceramics and glass. Alloys containing lithium are now commonly used in high performance parts of aircraft and in nuclear engineering. Most recently, it has been used in lithium batteries – particularly re-chargeable lithium-ion batteries.

Almost all of the lithium produced in Australia comes from Greenbushes, and all of that is sold to China. As by-products, the Greenbushes mine yields some potassium, sodium and phosphorous.

TITANIUM AND ZIRCON

Titanium is usually recovered from mineral sands, that is, from sands that contain a high level of ilmenite, rutile and zircon in the usual fine quartz. Ilmenite and rutile are the ores from which titanium is extracted. Such sands occur all around Australia but Western Australia, with its predominantly sandy coastal areas, has become the main source of the titanium ores mined in Australia. Tiwest – the company that operates a mine at Cooljarloo, nearby processing plants and a titanium pigment plant at Kwinana – claims to be 'the world's largest integrated titanium minerals production and manufacturing company.'[35]

35   See the Tiwest company's website at www.tiwest.com.au

The recovery of the zircon from Western Australia's mineral sands has become a significant element in Western Australia's economy and vital to the burgeoning Chinese heavy industry. Western Australia now produces about a third of the world's zirconium.

MANGANESE

Australia produces about 15% of world's manganese and is the third largest source of the metal. There are three mines in Australia; one, Woodie Woodie, is in Western Australia near Marble Bar.

The Woodie Woodie mine employs about 700 people, and each day almost 50 trucks set off from there on the 400 kilometre drive to Port Hedland loaded with manganese ore. Most of the manganese is shipped to China..

CHROMATE

Chromate and gold were first mined at Coobina, east of Newman, in 1924. The mines were never very profitable. In 2008 the global financial crisis resulted in a fall in the production of stainless steel and the price of chromate fell. The mines were closed down. They have since been reopened and ore is being exported to China.

** ** **

The natural assets described above have brought a considerable amount of wealth to Western Australia and have contributed to the rapid growth of the state's population. But in recent years, none of them has had as greater an influence on the state's economy as have iron ore and petroleum.

According to the Department of Mines and Petroleum 2008-2009 Statistics Digest, the top three commodities produced in Western Australia were:

Iron Ore – $33.6 billion
Crude Oil and Concentrates – $10.9 billion
Liquefied Natural Gas – $8.5 billion
Gold was fourth, earning $5.2 billion.

Iron ore and petroleum have become so important to the economy of Western Australia that they each deserve a chapter of their own. They will be dealt with separately in later chapters.

Chapter 10: *Dealing With Difficulties*

That the colony of Western Australia overcame its unpromising start was not just due to Britain's support during the convict era and the good fortune of finding rich deposits of gold and other minerals. The pioneers demonstrated resourcefulness and determination in overcoming the problems they faced in the difficult environment.

Major problems resulted from the locations chosen for the first two towns in the new colony; Fremantle on the south bank of the river and Perth on the north bank some 15 kilometres upstream. Between Perth and Fremantle – and for many kilometres further inland – there was no way to cross the river except by boat or by swimming. To travel from Fremantle to Perth settlers had either to travel up the river in a boat or cross it by horse ferry at Point Preston and then follow a sandy track through the bush to the Colony's capital. The Canning River, flowing into the Swan from the south near Perth, created a barrier to east-west travel on Fremantle's side of the river.

Despite its isolation, the peninsular at South Perth was chosen as the site for the Colony's first wind-powered flour mill. There, Governor Stirling laid the foundation stone for the mill in 1835. That position may have been convenient for farmers growing wheat beside the Canning River and the mill may have been more exposed to the westerly winds than it would have been had it been sited on the other side of the Swan where Perth was sheltered by Mount Eliza, but its isolation made the mill an easy target for leaders like Calyute who were bold enough to break and enter.

The old mill at South Perth has been carefully preserved – the Narrows Bridge and the Kwinana Freeway were constructed west of the most convenient position to avoid its demolition – and in 1990 it was placed on the register of the National Trust.

Ferries conveyed goods and people between Fremantle and Perth across the Swan River, but journeying between Perth and Guildford along the river was at first only possible in flat-bottomed boats as just east of Perth the river soaked its way through a mosquito-infested swamp. In 1831, the pioneers dredged a channel so that larger boats could be used to carry passengers and cargo between Perth and the settlements further up the Swan Valley. In less than four months a channel about 280 metres long, 9 metres wide and 4 metres deep was cut at the northern edge of the marshes.

The next challenge for the settlers was to link Perth with the areas south of the Swan by road. In 1841, a bridge with a span that could be raised to allow river traffic to pass was completed, but it could not be used until a causeway over the marshy flats had been constructed and that took a further two years.

The causeway and bridge linking the settlements north and south of the Swan – commonly called the Causeway – was badly damaged by the severe floods in 1862. Governor John Hampton ordered that the causeway be rebuilt considerably higher than the last time. He officially opened a new Causeway in 1867, and then proceeded upstream in a steamboat to open two newly constructed bridges – at Guildford and Helena. In 1866 convicts near Fremantle completed another bridge over the river. The Swan River was no longer such a significant impediment to the movements of the settlers.

As Perth's population grew, the Causeway became inadequate to handle the traffic crossing the river. By further dredging, a second channel was created at the south side of the swamp. The dredged material was used to create an artificial island, named Heirisson Island.[36] Two bridges then linked the island with the north and south shores of Swan River. That Causeway – as the new crossing was called, even though it was only two bridges and a short road across Heirisson Island – was opened for traffic in 1952.

Winter floods were almost an annual threat to the low-lying areas beside the Swan until the limestone bar and sand bank at the mouth of the river were removed during the development of Fremantle Harbour. Such floods are now extremely rare because the water in the river water

---

36   The mud flats included a few small islands that had been named Heirisson Islands in 1801 when a midshipman on the *Naturaliste* – Francois Heirisson explored the river from its mouth to the mud flats. He produced the first map of the river.

flows more easily out to sea. The Swan River, inland beyond Perth, is now a tidal estuary.

The first bridge over the Canning River was completed with convict labour in 1850. Those who designed it made the same mistake as did those responsible for the first causeway; no allowance was made for the Swan Valley's occasional floods. The deck of the Canning River Bridge was just two metres above the water in normal conditions, and it suffered serious damage during floods in 1862. Convicts were sent to work on a new bridge, this time with the deck four metres above water level. The bridge lasted until 1908 by which time it had deteriorated so much that it needed to be replaced. The present Canning River Bridge was built in 1939. It has since been widened, and the timber used in its construction has been replaced by steel and concrete.

There are now nineteen bridges over the Swan and Canning Rivers. The most celebrated of those is the Narrows Bridge from the foot of Mount Eliza to the South Perth Peninsular. When it was opened in 1954 it was said to be the largest pre-cast pre-stressed concrete bridge in the world. The foundations for such a heavy mass of concrete had to be solid, but on either side of the river the ground was mud to a depth of about 24 metres with sand for a further 12 metres below that. Dozens of piles were driven down to the bedrock and then filled with concrete. To provide access to the bridge a large area of the river had to be reclaimed with dredged material and then stabilised with thousands of tonnes of sand.

With Perth growing rapidly it was not long before the Narrows Bridge became an annoying bottleneck in the city's freeway system. It was the only link between the Kwinana Freeway to the south and the Mitchell freeway to the north. In 2001, a second bridge beside the first was opened, shortly followed by a railway bridge in 2005.

Ensuring an adequate water supply was –and still is – a challenge for the people of the Swan River settlement. Perth has a median average annual rainfall of about 750mm, and about 98% of that falls in the months from March to November. For the summer months the annual average total is only 8.5mm. To add to the difficulties posed by the annual summer drought, the rainfall is unreliable and Perth's summers average temperatures between 30 and 40 degrees.

Migrants from England's 'green and pleasant land', with its mild temperatures and proficient rainfall, would have found farming or cultivating extremely difficult in Perth's harsh climate. Their difficulties were compounded by the sandy soil of the coastal plain. The novelist, Anthony Trollope, visited Western Australia and noted that the soil around Perth was ideal – for hour glasses. Water poured onto crops in sandy soil rapidly soaks away, and sand lacks the nutrients necessary for growing strong crops. There was, however, one positive aspect of the sandy nature of the soil; water seeped down through the sand, collected above an impervious layer below, and could be recovered by sinking wells and bores. Today, almost 50% of the water supplied to Perth comes from underground natural reservoirs.

Early settlers in the Swan River area had to manage
during the summer drought with whatever water they had
stored, what they could recover from natural springs, or
what could be pumped up from below ground. There
were a number of swamps and lakes in low-lying areas
not far from the Perth township, but the water in them
was not suitable for drinking. Water-borne diseases were
a persistent problem in the settlement until 1891, when
the Victoria Dam was completed in the Darling Range.
Clean water was then piped down from the dam to a
reservoir on Mount Eliza and from there to the homes
and businesses of Perth. The Victoria Dam continued to
supply water to Perth until 1988 when it was found to be
in such poor condition that it was decided that it would be
best to demolish it. A new Victoria Dam replaced it, just
upstream from the old one.[37]

There are now eight major dams and nine smaller
pipehead dams that supply water to a large area in the
south-west of the state, but Perth's largest single source of
fresh water is a recently-constructed desalination plant.

37 See the Water Corporation website at www.watercorporation.com.au/D/
dams

Chapter 11: *Poisons And Pests*

While the townspeople in the Swan River settlements were dealing with their difficulties, farmers were facing serious problems of their own.

As far as graziers were concerned there was at least one advantage in Western Australia's isolation during the early years of the colony, and that was the fact that quarantine was rendered unnecessary. Infected stock would show clear symptoms of disease en route to the colony and animals with any fatal disease would die before reaching Fremantle. That did not mean that farmers and graziers in Western Australia had fewer problems than those in other parts of the world. The colony had enough of its own poisonous plants, bacteria and viruses, insects and native animal pests to make life extremely difficult.

The native animals of Australia have learned what plants to avoid eating or have evolved digestive systems that can handle any toxicity in the plants that they eat. The sheep, cattle and horses brought to the colony had neither the knowledge of what not to eat nor immunity from the poisonous plants of Australia. Many of the *Gastrolobium* family contain the 1080 poison used for the control of the rabbit plague. The settlers gave names to various species of that family such as 'York Road Poison', 'Champion Bay Poison' and the 'Hutt River Poison'. The *Oxylobium* group (called 'Box Poison') are just as toxic. Zamia *(Macrozamia riedlei)* causes paralysis of the hindquarters of cattle. *Crotalaria*, or rattlepod, a shrub foundin the Kimberley causes the 'walking disease' that compels horses to walk – in straight lines, regardless of obstacles. Those and other poisonous plants in Western Australia caused extremely serious stock losses as cattle, sheep and horses grazed on the native vegetation. It took settlers a long time to identify which plants were killing their animals, and then the only way to remove poisonous plant from their property was by hand-grubbing, ploughing or burning.

Graziers were able to protect stock on their properties by clearing them of all poisonous plants, but droving animals to a new location remained hazardous. In 1835, flocks of sheep were driven from the Swan Valley to the new farms around York and there were substantial losses as a result of the animals eating the poisonous bushes along the way. In 1840, a large mob of sheep and bullocks was driven overland from Albany to the Swan Valley, but about 250 sheep and over 50 of the cattle died of poisoning. When the Kojonup area was first settled in the 1840s some farmers suffered almost total loss of their flocks because of the prevalence of poisonous plants in the area.

As well as poisonous plant, sheep farmers suffered losses due to pests. The two worst were scab mites (*Psoroptes ovis*) and blow-flies.

Scab mites were brought into Australia by infected sheep and spread rapidly across the continent. The mites pierce the skin of the sheep, causing a dermatitis that ruins fleeces and causes a high mortality rate among an infected flock. The only way to deal with scab infestations was by plunge-dipping every sheep in a bath of nicotine and sulphuric acid. That was time-consuming, costly, and often ineffective as the mites are capable of surviving for days in sheds, on fences or on the clothing of farm workers and are therefore difficult to eliminate.

The graziers in Western Australia were able to profit from the experience of those in New South Wales. There, in 1832, the Government enacted Australia's first legislation to control animal disease. Under New South Wales laws inspectors were appointed with power to inspect, seize and destroy animals infected with scab mites. The inspectors had the right to demand that any infected flocks were kept under supervision and enclosed at night. Gradually, graziers were able to reduce the incidence of scab mite infections. By 1896 scab mites had been completely eliminated in Australia – a remarkable achievement considering that the disease still remains a serious problem in many other parts of the world.

Scab mites were far easier to deal with than blow flies. Flies are impossible to eradicate. Strike by blow-flies can kill a sheep within a few days. The fly deposits its maggots in the wool, and the maggots then proceed to feed on the sheep's living tissue. According to the Western Australian Department of Agriculture, blow flies were causing an annual loss of about $160 million to the Australian wool industry during the first half of the twenty-first century.[38]

To minimise stock losses from blow-fly strikes, the pioneer graziers were forced to undertake frequent inspections, crutching, drenching, and jetting with insecticides. There was no other solution until the practices of mulesing and tail-stripping were introduced in the 1930s. Those practices significantly reduced the stock deaths by fly strikes, but mulesing had lately been condemned by animal rights groups. Today, the focus is on breeding sheep less vulnerable to fly-strike. Since the dung beetle was released in 1968, there has been a significant reduction in the number of flies in some areas. The beetles seem to have been particularly effective in the tropical north and in the Busselton district.

Among the problems that grain growers faced in the Western Australian environment was the defence of their crops against raids by kangaroos, emus and flocks of other native birds. Fences around paddocks were not particularly helpful. A common response to crop losses caused by native animals was to shoot as many of the offenders as possible. Conservation of native fauna was not a priority with the pioneers.

The first restriction on killing native fauna was the Kangaroo Ordinance of 1853. This was intended to reduce conflict between indigenous Australians and settlers who were slaughtering kangaroos for their skins. It did not limit the right of landholders and aboriginals to kill animals for meat, but it did place a punitive export duty on kangaroo hides. There is no reason to believe that farmers did not

38 See the Western Australian Department of Agriculture and Food website at www.agric.wa.gov.au/PC_90050

continue to shoot kangaroos just because they considered them to be pests.

The government next passed the first Game Act of 1874, which was primarily concerned with regulating the game that had been imported for hunting. It recognised that for some species there should be a closed season.

In 1892, amendments to the Game Act classified kangaroos and Tammar wallabies as 'game' and therefore enabled them to receive some protection. The act also proclaimed reservations where no animals could be taken without government permission. The first of such reservations was proclaimed in 1899. Even in proclaimed reservations bona fide settlers and aboriginals were still free to kill animals for food but not for sale.

The first major step towards wildlife conservation was the Fauna Protection Act of 1950. Under the act, all wild vertebrate animals in the state were classified as fauna; all fauna was protected unless a specific exemption was allowed by the government. It became an offence for anyone to trap or kill any fauna that is native to Australia or that periodically migrates to Australia. The only exception to that rule was the dingo. The Department of Conservation was given power to grant licences to cull species if it considered that to be necessary.[39]

Vertebrate animals did not cause as much loss to the Colony's grain growers in the nineteenth century as did weevils and rust.

The Greenough area seemed, at first, to be destined to be the granary of the colony. The first wheat crop was

---

39   The author is indebted to R.I.T. Prince for providing a copy of his excellent paper on 'Exploitation of Kangaroos and Wallabies in Western Australia' prepared for the Western Australian Wildlife Research Centre in 1984.

sown there in 1852 and by 1860, an area of over 3,000 acres called the Flats was dedicated to growing wheat. In 'the Flats' there were three mills producing flour. The yield was so high that there was enough to export, and the first shipment of grain for England was loaded onto a ship at Geraldton. The entire shipment was ruined by weevils before it reached England.

Weevils could be defeated by careful hygiene – disinfecting equipment and storing grain in clean, sealed bins – but there were worse problems to come for the Greenough farmers. In 1868, Red Rust destroyed practically every crop in the district. Red Rust became endemic to the area, and kept spreading. Red Rust, cyclones and then devastating floods in 1880 spelled the end of Greenough's significance as a wheat-growing area. It was not until William Farrer developed a rust-resistant strain of wheat in 1901 – named Federation – that farmers in Australia were able to grow wheat crops that were impervious to Red Rust. Since then, wheat-growing has become one of Western Australia's major exports. Australia is one of the top five wheat-exporting countries of the world and Western Australia grows more than half of the wheat exported.

Farmers and graziers were equally affected by arguably the worst pest to invade Western Australia – the rabbit. Indigenous animals such as dingoes and kangaroos may have caused some stock and crop losses, but rabbits proved to be far more destructive than both.

Rabbits were introduced to Australia via Geelong in 1859 and from there they spread at an incredible rate. The

Nullabor proved to be no barrier to their progress westward. By 1894 large numbers of rabbits were found around Eucla and the surrounding area was soon stripped of vegetation. Even prior to this, some rabbits had made their way into the west of the colony. They were sighted at Cheynes Beach in 1887 and at Northampton in 1893. They were even seen on the Abrolhos Islands where it was said some had been left to feed any shipwrecked sailors.

In 1901 there was a Royal Commission regarding the rabbit problem and it was decided that a rabbit-proof fence would be erected to halt the invasion from the east. A fence was built from Burracoppin to Bedford Harbour but by the time it was finished the rabbits were well west of it. Another fence was hastily erected from Wiluna to near Bremer Bay. However, it was not long until rabbits had breached this fence too. By 1930, rabbits had become a serious plague throughout the farming areas of the state – depriving stock of sustenance, destroying native vegetation, ruining crops and pock-marking the landscape with burrows.

Federal Government action was required to deal with the situation. The poison 1080 was recommended by the Agricultural Protection Board and it was used with some success. But the major breakthrough in the fight against the rabbit plague came with the introduction of the myxomatosis virus. It was first introduced into the wild rabbit population by the release of infected rabbits in Western Australia in 1951. The disease spread rapidly. Within five years it was estimated that the rabbit population had been reduced to 10% of what it had been at its peak.

When myxomatosis began to lose its effectiveness the calicivirus was introduced into the rabbit population. There are still rabbits in Western Australia, but they are not in such great numbers to be regarded as pests.

The latest pest to invade Western Australia is the cane toad. One was caught in Kununurra in 2009. It seems that significant numbers of the toads are now in the state's north and are already posing a danger to native fauna. In 2011 they were responsible for the deaths of four crocodiles in the east Kimberley – the crocodiles had unwisely eaten poisonous toads. It remains to be seen if they can be prevented from spreading further; all the attempts to stop the spread of the cane toad in the east have failed.

The measure of protection from exotic diseases and pests afforded by Western Australia's isolation has gradually evaporated as transport speeds have increased. Quarantine stations now provide the only protection at the border on the Eyre Highway and at airports and ports.

Chapter 12:

Education – State And Church

In the chaotic first year of the Swan River settlement there was no provision for the education of children. This is not surprising considering that there was almost no provision in England for the education of children whose parents could not afford to send them to a Public School. In 1807 Samuel Whitbread had presented a Bill to the House of Commons that intended to make parishes responsible for providing every child between the ages of 7 and 14 with two years of schooling. His scheme was never a great success, but the desirability of providing education for all children in order to reduce crime and pauperism gradually gained wider acceptance in the early decades of the nineteenth Century. As a result, the Colonial Treasury decided to support the establishment of a school in the new colony of Western Australia.

In 1830 the first school in Perth – called the Colonial School because it was partly financed by the Colonial Office – admitted its first pupils. Parents were required to pay fees to cover part of the cost of their children's education. The school was not well supported and the number of pupils attending varied considerably, but it managed to survive for about eight years. For the latter part of that time it occupied a building that had been erected specifically to house it. When the Colonial School was closed down due to lack of support, the school house became the Colonial Hospital.

In 1846 an attempt was made to re-establish the Colonial School, though the ten boys and three girls attended irregularly. The Headmaster gained a reputation for being incompetent.

Major Irwin, then Governor of Western Australia, decided something had to be done about the lack of good education for the children in the colony. In 1847 he set up an Education Committee with two sub-committees – one of men and another of women – and ordered them to investigate the situation and recommend remedies.

The Committee found that there were 230 children of settlers attending schools in the colony. Thirteen were attending the Colonial School, and the rest were being taught in private schools. Five of the private schools only catered for about 20 pupils and were run by women – presumably in their own homes. The Roman Catholic Church which, in New South Wales had ruled that Roman Catholic children should not be educated at secular government schools, had one school attended by about 30 boys and another attended by about 60 girls, most of whom were Protestants. The Methodists had a co-educational school catering for about 40. Some 170 children, as the Committee estimated, were receiving no education other than what they might be given at home. The Committee did not investigate what was happening regarding the education of aboriginal children.

The Education Committee then set about establishing two new schools – Perth Girls' School and Perth Boys' School. Their objectives were stated as the provision of an *education for boys equal to that obtainable at a good English Grammar School, and for girls such a one as a respectable middle class person would endeavour to secure for his daughter in England.*[40] Whether or not the Committee succeeded in doing that, its two schools did soon gain a good reputation. Within a few years almost all those private schools, except those run by the Roman Catholic Church, had lost their pupils to the two new government schools.

At first neither the boys' school nor the girls' school had its own premises. The building that had housed the old Colonial School was being used as the Colony's hospital. Classes for the boys were held in the Court House, which meant that they had to be taught outside or given a holiday when the Court was in session. The girls were taught in rooms owned by the Methodist Church. In 1850 the Boys' School also moved to the rooms owned by the Methodists, but after just two years numbers forced the boys to move again, this time to the Mechanics Institute.

The number of pupils attending Perth Boys' School and Perth Girls' School increased every year until the government decided that the time had come for the town to erect proper school buildings. The Colonial Secretary, William Sanford, was given the task of preparing the

---

40 See page ten of the annual report of the Education Board 1855 quoted by John K. Ewers in a paper prepared for the WA Historical Society Journal December 1947.

basic design for a Boy's School and the detailed plans were drawn up by Richard Jewell. Sanford and Jewell were clearly admirers of the Gothic style of architecture; the building they designed is like a Gothic-revival parish church. Unlike many of the buildings in Perth of the time, the Boys' School was constructed to last, with walls of limestone blocks that were conveyed from Fremantle by boat. It is still well-preserved and is currently being used as a café. It is owned by the National Trust and has been entered in the State Register of Heritage Places.

In 1854 the Boys' School moved into their new premises and there it remained for about forty years. The girls were provided with their own school building on Pier Street near the Deanery.

By 1871, the Legislative Council had passed the Education Act that made attendance at school compulsory for all children between the ages of 6 and 14 who lived within five kilometres of a school. That resulted in a substantial increase in the numbers of children attending the town's schools. It was decided to erect a substantial two-storied building in James Street and to locate there both the Boys' and Girls' schools. The first lessons in the new Perth Boys' and Girls' School were conducted there in 1896.

For forty years boys and girls were educated in that James Street building. In 1936 the girls were moved out and Perth Boys' School, which was called Perth Boys' High School after 1946, occupied the building until 1958 when all secondary school students were directed to co-educational suburban schools. The James Street school is now classified as a heritage building and is occupied by the Perth Institute of Contemporary Arts.

The girls were divided into two streams; those hoping to go on to tertiary education were directed to the new Perth Girls' School which had been built on the corner of Wellington Street and Plain Street; while those intending to join the workforce after leaving school were sent to Perth Central Girls' School. The Perth Central Girls' School later came to be known as Girdlestone High School. It was housed in a new building next to Perth Boys' High School.

Perth Girls' School was built on part of the Chinese and Presbyterian sections of the old East Perth Cemetery. Eventually, even more of the cemetery was given over to providing tennis courts for the girls. The Chinese and Presbyterians in Perth may not have been happy, but the building erected for the girls is certainly very impressive. It is in the 'Inter War Stripped Classical style – a rare use of a style more often associated with parliamentary buildings',[41] and is now classified as a heritage building. It is currently occupied by the Police Department.

It seems that the ambitious goals set by Education Committee for Perth's schools did not apply to schools in Albany. Frances Legare, a retired whaler with no training as a teacher, was given charge of the Albany school for girls in 1853. Thomas Palmer, who was serving a ten year term of transportation for forgery, was employed to teach at the Albany boys' school. The Committee cannot have been greatly concerned with what was happening regarding the education of Australian aboriginals. John McKail, who had been banished to Albany for shooting

41 See the Heritage Council of Western Australia's website at register.heritage.gov.wa.au

an aborigine in Fremantle, was put in charge of Albany's school for indigenous children.[42]

At least Albany did have a school for aboriginal children. Otherwise it was only the Christian missionaries who made any attempt to educate the native children in the nineteenth century.

The Church of England's Western Australian Missionary Society was established in 1836 by C.F. Irwin, a cousin of Governor Stirling. It purchased a site near Guildford, part of which is still vested in the Anglican Church and known as 'Swanleigh'. The Society's first missionary, the Reverend Giustiniani, built a home there for himself and a building in which to educate aboriginal children. After just two years he went back to England. The Reverend William Mitchell then took over the mission. He brought with him his family and their governess, Anne Breeze. In 1838 Mitchell and Breeze set up a mission school at Middle Swan where they educated aboriginal children and some children of settlers in the district.

The mission school that the Reverend Giustiniani had founded at Swanleigh was reopened by the Reverend Abraham Jones in 1841. That same year Reverend George King opened a 'Native School' at Fremantle. Two years later Mitchell founded a second school in Middle Swan and Reverend Postlethwaite opened a school for children of settlers and aboriginals in the Upper Swan. Those early mission schools were largely dependent upon the zeal of the founders and most did not last for long. King's Native School was the exception.

42 'J Dowson. *Old Albany*. Albany Chamber of Commerce and Industry 2008 @ p 208.

Archdeacon John Wollaston acquired 60 acres near Middleton Beach, Albany and arranged for King's school to be relocated there. He turned to Anne Breeze for help running it as she had moved to Albany, after marrying a local resident, Henry Camfield. In 1852 Anne and her husband took upon themselves the responsibility of managing what was called the 'Albany Native Institution'. One of its primary functions soon became caring for sick and orphaned aboriginal children.

The Camfields kept the Albany Native Institution going until Anne retired in 1871. When there were no funds to allow it to continue to function in its own premises, they took aboriginal girls into their own home. In order to accommodate more girls, they built an annexe containing a classroom, a kitchen and accommodation for eight children. By 1868 they had taken in fifty-five children. Anne Camfield fed and clothed them while teaching reading and writing, the Christian faith and European standards of hygiene. She also equipped them for employment in the homes of the settlers by teaching them how to perform domestic tasks. One of her students even learned how to play the piano.

The Institution was largely financed by the Camfields themselves. Local people were encouraged to visit the Institution and to give donations to help with the costs. It has been noted that eleven girls died while in the care of the Camfields, but that was almost certainly due to the fact that many girls were very sick when they had arrived at the Institution.

The numbers in Camfields' care dwindled during Anne's last active years due to the fact that there were fewer aboriginals in the area. European diseases had severe consequences for the indigenous population. Smallpox and measles had ravaged the tribes around Albany, and a great many died in an outbreak of influenza in 1845.

When the Camfields retired, Bishop Hale – the first Bishop of the Church of England in Western Australia – brought their few remaining pupils to Perth to attend a school he had established for indigenous children. He had, at his own expense, built a two-storied house in Saint George's Terrace to accommodate what he called the 'Native and Half Caste Institution'. The Institution continued to care for children there until 1888 when Hale's successor, Bishop Parry, moved the children to the 'Swan Native and Half Caste Mission' at Middle Swan.

After her husband died in 1872, Anne moved to Perth so that she could be near the girls that had been in her care. Camfield House still stands at the corner of Crossman and Serpentine Roads in Albany and is listed by the National Trust. The annexe they built to accommodate extra girls was damaged by fire and was subsequently demolished.

Dom Rosendo Salvado and Dom Joseph Serra of the Benedictine Order, pioneer missionaries working among the Indigenous Australians at the same time as Anne Camfield, have a far more impressive memorial: the monastery at New Norcia.

Dom Salvado and Dom Serra arrived in Perth on the ship that brought out the first Roman Catholic Bishop of Western Australia, John Brady, in 1846. They set off, with three companions, to establish a mission to the aboriginals about a hundred kilometres north of Perth but the support of those three companions was soon lost. One died and the others' health prevented their continued work in the mission. Dom Salvado and Dom Serra received no financial help from the Diocese – Bishop Brady had been given a diocese with virtually no assets – but with help of volunteers they erected the first buildings of a new settlement they called New Norcia after Nursia, the birthplace of Benedict.

Word spread among the local aboriginals that the Benedictine monks were willing to help by providing food and medicine. They increasingly looked to the two monks for aid, and soon the monks were being trusted to care for and educate aboriginal boys.

The New Norcia mission endured years of struggle until, in 1859, it was granted independence from the Diocese of Perth and Dom Salvado was able to take charge. Under his guidance, the mission grew to become a town with houses, workshops, an orphanage and a flour mill. After 54 years of devoted service to his mission at New Norcia, Dom Salvado died in 1900 aged 86.

Matthew Blagden Hale, the first Anglican Bishop of Western Australia, was a significant figure in education for the children of white settlers as well as native Australians. He, like Bishop Brady, found himself in charge of a new diocese with no accumulated funds but he did not allow that to hinder his plans to make his diocese a contributor to the development of education in Western Australia. He had money of his own, and he used it to establish a school and hire teachers. It was many years before he was reimbursed by the Church.

While working in the Diocese of Adelaide, Hale had become familiar with the contribution Saint Peter's Collegiate School was making to education in South Australia. He arrived in Perth determined to establish a similar secondary school for boys in his diocese. In Saint George's Terrace there was a building designed by Richard Jewell and was known as the Cloisters. Hale purchased it in 1858 and, with teachers he had employed, began educating sons of settlers. The Cloisters still stand at 202 Saint George's Terrace.

The Bishop's Collegiate School was not a great success. It never attracted more than about twenty students. Undaunted by the difficulties he was facing with his Collegiate School, Hale offered to pay the fare of an English woman to come to teach young ladies at a sister school. However, he received only one application for admission to his proposed school for young ladies, so he abandoned his plans and was compelled to pay the teacher's fare back to England.

In the end, Hale resigned himself to the fact that the Western Australian colony was not ready to support a secondary boys' college. In 1872 he wrote,

'There is no such thing as convincing the people that education pays. Making their sons messengers on a sheep station pays and that settles the question.... Parents won't use the school, so it's no use to keep it struggling on.'[43]

The Bishop closed down his Collegiate School in 1872, but within eighteen months a group of influential

43 A.S. Robin, *M.B. Hale – The Life of an Australian Pioneer Bishop,* Hawthorn Press, 1976.

citizens had set up a new school in the Bishop's classrooms – with his permission. Called 'The High School', it had no connection with the Church or with Bishop Hale, but it later changed its name to 'Hale School' and claimed continuity with the school that the Bishop had founded in 1858. To justify that claim it is able to point out that it used Bishop Hale's classrooms and most of the boys in its first year had been pupils at the Bishop's Collegiate School.

Despite the disappointments he had suffered in his attempts to establish the Collegiate School, Hale went ahead with building his 'Native and Half Caste Institution' in 1872. It continued to cater for 'native and half caste' children in the premises on Saint George's Terrace until Bishop Parry moved it to Middle Swan in 1888.

In 1875 Hale accepted the position of Bishop of Brisbane. During his time in Western Australia the number of Anglican clergy increased from just eight to 17 and the number of parish churches rose from 14 to 28. It seems he had more success with the administration of his diocese than he had with introducing private school education.

The education system in Western Australia is now virtually the same as that in every other state of Australia. Throughout Australia there is free and compulsory education for all children in state schools and also a thriving private school system. With people increasingly likely to move interstate in the course of employment, the various state education authorities have recognised the need for all states to have similar curricula and steady progress is being made towards reaching that goal.

Chapter 13: *Overcoming Isolation*

Perth is the world's most isolated capital city. The nearest other capital – Adelaide – is some 2,700 kilometres away. For decades those living in Western Australia could only communicate with people in other major centres of civilisation by means of letters conveyed by sea. The development of the telegraph system first enabled the people of Perth to be linked to the outside world by a more rapid means of communication.

By 1845 there were telegraph services operating in U.S.A. and Britain, and by the end of the 1850s telegraph wires had connected the major cities in eastern Australia from Brisbane to Adelaide. Western Australia was slow to adopt the new technology. It was not until 1869 that its first telegraph service connected Perth with Fremantle. A further eight years passed before there was a telegraphic link between Perth and the Eastern States.

Discussions between the South Australian and Western Australian governments regarding a telegraph line between Adelaide and Perth commenced in 1860. But it took no fewer than seventeen years for an agreement to be reached and the construction of the telegraphic link to be completed.

The South Australian Government undertook the erection and maintenance of the telegraph line from Adelaide to Eucla, while the Western Australian Government accepted responsibility for the line from Eucla to Perth. The route chosen for the telegraph line followed, to a large extent, the route taken by Edward John Eyre on his trek from Adelaide to Albany in 1841. This meant that it was never far from the southern coastline so that men and materials could easily be transported to the line by ship. The thousands of poles and the kilometres of wire needed were carried by sea to points as close as possible to where work was in progress. From there they were hauled by horses to the line, often after negotiating the steep cliffs of the coastline along the Great Australian Bight.

The South Australians made a better job of their section of line than the Western Australians. The South Australian section had tubular steel poles and copper wire. The Western Australia Government opted for cheaper wooden poles and steel wire. Fire, white ants and decay attacked the wooden poles while the steel wire had a tendency to snap due to the extremes of temperature. In 1897 the wooden poles were replaced by steel poles, and later the steel wire was replaced by copper.

Relay stations were placed at various places along the telegraph line to receive and re-transmit signals, so ensuring that messages were not lost by fading away over the vast distances covered by the line. At first there were just two relay stations in Western Australia between Perth and

Eucla – at Albany and Israelite Bay – but it was soon found necessary to place additional relays at Eyre, Esperance and Bremer Bay. At Eucla, Western Australian operators passed or received messages from across the border.

Telegraph cables had connected Britain to Darwin and Darwin to Adelaide in 1872. In 1877, when Perth became linked by telegraph to Adelaide, Western Australians had the means to communicate not only with all the other Australian capital cities but also with London. The telegraph line connecting Adelaide to Perth via Eucla and Albany continued to be an important link with the outside world until 1927, when a new line beside the Trans-continental railway rendered it superfluous.

In 1901, Guillermo Marconi succeeded in transmitting a message in Morse code across the Atlantic without any connecting wires. The days of telegraph lines were clearly numbered, but the old technology was not quickly discarded. There were no less than 161 telegraph stations in Western Australia in 1900, and they continued to provide a valued service until 1989 when the Perth telegraph office was finally closed down.

* *  * *

It was the development of the telephone that made the telegraph service obsolete. In 1876 Alexander Graham Bell was awarded the first patent for the electric telephone. The world rapidly embraced the new technology, and the first telephone exchange in Australia was installed in Melbourne in 1880. Perth's first telephone service began operations in 1887 with 17 subscribers. The next year, a Fremantle exchange was initiated with just 9 subscribers. At first the telephone service in Western Australia allowed only conversations between people within the state. It was not until well into the twentieth century that it became possible for Western Australians to speak by telephone with people in other Australian states or countries.

Before Federation each state had its own telephone system. In 1901 the Commonwealth Constitution made the control of posts, telegraphic, telephonic and all other communication services one of the responsibilities of the Commonwealth Government. The Postmaster General's Department (the PMG) was established to administer all telephone, telegraph and postal services, and it set to work to connect all parts of the Commonwealth.

Telephonic transmissions – like telegraph messages – become weaker as they travel over long distances but repeater stations, like those that had been established along the telegraph line, were not appropriate for telephone calls. The technology to enable satisfactory long distance telephone calls was gradually improved. Sydney and Melbourne were connected by a trunk line in 1907. Adelaide and Brisbane were linked into the trunk line system in 1914 and 1923 respectively. Perth was not connected until 1930.

Until 1993 the provision of telephone services throughout Australia was a monopoly under the control of the Commonwealth agency known, throughout its history, by a variety of names, and finally became the Telstra Corporation. The Government then decided to allow one company – Optus – to compete with Telstra. Before long other companies were entering the market and the competition resulted in a radical transformation of communication. Perth's geographical isolation is now of little consequence.

**  **

A vital step in ending Perth's isolation was the building of the Transcontinental Railway. When discussions were taking place regarding the formation of the Commonwealth of Australia, some Western Australian politicians were unhappy at the prospect of surrendering some of their power to a federal government. A rail connection between Perth and the eastern states, to be built at the Commonwealth Government's expense, was mentioned during negotiations as one of the benefits that would flow from Federation.

After Federation, the Commonwealth Government did not take long to begin surveying the route for the Transcontinental Railway. An initial analysis of the route was completed in 1907. At that stage Kalgoorlie was a thriving city and the source of most of Western Australia's wealth, so it was decided to run the line from Kalgoorlie across the Nullarbor Plain instead of following the route of the old telegraph line through Albany.

The South Australian and Western Australian Governments agreed to grant to the Commonwealth the land on which the line was to be built. Commonwealth Railways was incorporated in 1912 and that same year work was begun on a standard gauge line from Port Augusta towards Perth. The next year Western Australian workers began laying the track from Kalgoorlie towards the east. The First World War did not delay the project and the railway lines from met and were joined in October 1917.

There were, at the time, three different railway gauges in Australia. New South Wales had adopted the European standard of 1435 mm. Victoria, and parts of South Australia, had the wider Irish gauge of 1600 mm. Queensland, Western Australia, Tasmania and parts of South Australia had the narrow 1067 mm. gauge. As a result, interstate rail travel for many years meant changing trains at state borders. The inconvenience of changing trains became a problem that the military faced when transporting troops and equipment around the country by rail during the Second World War. It was this potentially troublesome hindrance that caused the Commonwealth Government to take some steps to improve the situation. However, it was not until 1970 that passengers could travel from Perth to Sydney on the same train that ran on a standard gauge line all the way.

Only one track was laid between Kalgoorlie and Port Augusta which meant that when trains had to pass one had to wait on a siding. Sidings were constructed at regular intervals along the track, with a railway employee housed permanently beside each of them to be available to operate the switch. Most of these remote settlements have now been abandoned as train drivers now change the switch themselves via remote control.

The lack of water on the Nullarbor Plain meant that steam trains had to carry all the water they would need for one particular 400 kilometre section of the journey. For steam engines about half of the load being conveyed over that section had to be water. The switch to diesel-electric locomotives solved the problem.

One advantage of the treeless, flat terrain of the Nullarbor Plain was that it allowed a section of the line to be straight for 463 kilometres. It is said to be the longest straight stretch of rail in the world.

During the First World War the design and construction of aircraft for combat improved markedly. When the War ended there were many young men who had learned to fly in the various Air Forces of the combatants and enjoyed doing it, and there were factories producing aircraft reliable enough to be used commercially.

Recognising that aircraft would be bound to be important not only for the defence of the country but also for civilian transport, the Australian Government passed the country's first Air Navigation Act in 1920 and set up a Civil Aviation Authority to promote and control aviation in Australia. The first person to be granted a commercial pilot's licence by the Civil Aviation Authority was a Western Australian, Norman Brearley.

Brearley had been a pilot in the Royal Flying Corps who had been shot down, suffering bullet wounds to both of his lungs. After the War, Brearley purchased two Avro 504 aircraft and for a time made money by taking people on joy flights. His aircraft were kept at the property of

Michael Durack in Adelaide Terrace, and he used Langley Park as his airfield.

Brearley formed a company called Western Australian Airways and it tendered for a government-subsidised mail and passenger service between Geraldton and Derby. It was awarded the contract, so Brearley then imported six Bristol Type 26 two-seater biplanes and advertised for pilots who had been members of the Royal Flying Corps. One of those who replied was Charles Kingsford Smith.

While Brearley was setting up his airline in Western Australia, William Hudson Fysh, Paul McGinness and Fergus McMaster were establishing Queensland and Northern Territory Air Services (QANTAS) based at Winton in Queensland.

On 3 December 1921 Western Australia's first air service was formally launched in the presence of the Governor with a rally in the Perth Town Hall followed by demonstrations of flying at Langley Park. After the demonstrations, three planes of the Western Australian Airways fleet set off for Geraldton. After a brief stopover at Geraldton, the three took off to pioneer the service to Derby. One of them developed engine problems and was forced to land. Another stalled while circling over the grounded aircraft and crashed. The pilot and the mechanic accompanying him were killed.

Despite that initial setback, Western Australian Airways prospered. Its regular route from Geraldton to Derby involved stops at Carnarvon, Onslow, Roebourne, Port Hedland and Broome. People in those isolated towns could send mail or freight – or even fly as passengers – over vast distances in a fraction of the time it would previously have taken. Before long, Brearley had begun a regular service from Perth to Geraldton. In 1928 he was awarded a contract to carry passengers and freight between Perth and Adelaide. The aircraft used by Western Australian Airways on that route were De Havilland 66 Hercules that cruised at just 95 knots (about 170 kilometres per hour) and had to land to refuel at Forrest and at Kalgoorlie. At Kalgoorlie the passengers had to spend the night at a hotel.

Charles Kingsford Smith was a pilot with Western Australian Airways for just two years. After a dispute with Brearley regarding pay and conditions, Kingsford Smith and another pilot, Keith Anderson, left the company and set up a trucking business based in Carnarvon. The Gascoyne Transport Company, as their firm was named, won a contract for the mail run from Meekatharra to Carnarvon and was reasonably profitable, but Kingsford Smith and Anderson were not content being grounded. After just two years in the trucking business they sold the Gascoyne Transport Company, purchased two aircraft from Brearley and flew them to Sydney where they started a business they named Interstate Flying Services. That flight from Perth to Sydney took over four days. Air transport was not a serious competitor for the railways. It was more expensive, more hazardous and not a great deal faster.

The development of larger, faster and more reliable aircraft brought more customers to the airlines. An airport was established at Maylands, and by 1934 there were three airline companies based there. In 1936 Brearley sold Western Australian Airways to Adelaide Airways and it soon became absorbed into Australian National Airways (ANA). Western Australia's own airline had lasted just fifteen years.

In 1938, MacRobertson Miller Aviation began a service from Perth to Darwin in addition to a weekly flight from Perth to Adelaide, this meant larger aircraft and increased air traffic. Maylands airfield was proving to be inadequate, so the State Government decided to establish a larger airfield at Guildford. Before civil airlines could use the new Guildford aerodrome it was taken over by the military to become the base for Perth's air defences throughout the Second World War.

Despite objections from the military, in 1944 the government allowed Qantas and ANA to use Guildford Airport. In May, an ANA DC-3 landed there, collecting freight and passengers and set off again for Adelaide. The next month, a Qantas-modified Liberator bomber initiated the Kangaroo Service, flying out of Guildford to Ceylon via Exmouth.

After the War, airlines rapidly assumed a major role in transport in and out of Perth. Aircraft could convey perishables, manufactured goods, mail and passengers to and from the eastern states in a matter of hours while transport by rail took days. Road transport was never a competitor because there was no decent road between Perth and Adelaide.

The arrival of the jet age was an important step in ending Perth's isolation. Jet-powered aircraft complete the journey from Perth to Sydney in four hours. Kingsford Smith and Anderson had taken over four days to cover the same distance.

The number of passengers travelling through Perth Airport has, in recent years, increased by 7.5% per annum. The airlines have not only contributed to overcoming the Perth's isolation from the other major cities of the world, but for many Western Australians they play an important role in the normal course of their employment. 'Fly-in fly-out' employment contracts are now popular in the mining and petroleum industries. Many workers work long hours on an oil rig or at a mine in some remote location for a fortnight or so, then fly home to Perth to spend a week with their families before flying back to work again.

**  **

The Eyre Highway between Western Australia and Adelaide had its origins in the track that was used to construct and service the old telegraph line, and owed much to the explorations of Edward John Eyre. It was not until 1941 that work was begun to create what might be considered to be a proper road from Norseman to Port Augusta. At first, the road was unsealed, dusty and potholed. Though an unsatisfactory way to travel, it did contain the longest straight stretch of road in the world – 146.6 kilometres.

Despite the condition of the road, traffic on the Eyre Highway increased until the South Australian and Western Australian Governments had to recognise that it had become an important interstate highway. Work was begun to seal the road, but the last section – in South Australia – was not sealed until 1976. It is now a busy, vital link between Western Australia and the rest of the country, and is still the only sealed road that crosses the border.

Chapter 14:

Towards Self Government And Federation

The British Government had learnt from the trouble caused by the imposition of taxation without representation it had experienced with the Thirteen Colonies in North America and took care to respond to any reasonable aspirations regarding self-government in the Australian Colonies. The free citizens of New South Wales were first granted a say in the government of their colony in 1823 when a council was established to advise the governor. The members of that council were appointed by the Crown. Two years later an Executive Council, again nominated, not elected, was set up and the governor was instructed to act on its advice. In 1828 the Executive Council had doubled the number of members. In 1843, once convicts transportation virtually finished, New South Wales was granted representative government. The enlarged New South Wales Legislative Council consisted of 36 members – 12 nominated by the Crown, 24 elected by landowners and householders (men only).

Tasmania was made a separate colony in 1825, and by 1855 it was granted self-government. Its constitution was similar to that of New South Wales. The same year Victoria became a separate colony with its own parliament. South Australia, though it was settled after Western Australia, received its own constitution as a self-governing colony in 1857. Queensland was granted its independence from New South Wales and responsible government four years later. This left Western Australia as the only one of the six Australian colonies without its own democratically elected government.

For the first two years after its establishment, the Colony of Western Australia was administered by Lieutenant Governor Stirling who was an autocrat answerable only to his superiors in Britain. On 1 November 1830 an Order-in-Council had been issued 'for the establishment of a Legislative Council to make all necessary laws and to constitute all necessary courts for the peace, order and good government of the settlement' but it was not until 7 February 1832 that a Legislative Council of four nominated members – all government officials selected by the governor – was convened for the first time.

The Legislative Council's powers were strictly limited. Any law made in Western Australia had to first be proposed by the governor and it could be disallowed by the Secretary of State. In 1839 the Council was doubled in size as an additional four citizens, nominated by the governor, took their seats.

Any further progress towards self-government for Western Australia was rendered unlikely when, in 1850, the colony agreed to become a destination for convicts sentenced to transportation. While it was accepting convicts and financial support from the British Government, the state was not entitled to the same independent status as the eastern states. In 1865 a petition for self-government submitted by citizens of the colony to the British Government accomplished nothing.

When transportation to Western Australia ended in 1868, politically-minded citizens in the colony had reason to expect that it would be granted a constitution similar to those that applied to the other Australian colonies. A petition was submitted to the British Government asking that the members of the Legislative Council be elected by the citizens of the colony.

Nathaniel Ogle, in his 1839 *The Colony of Western Australia – A Manual for Immigrants*, stated that *'When fifty thousand inhabitants are reported by census, they can frame a constitution for themselves, under the Crown of England.'*[44] He did not cite his authority for that, but it may well have been true. In 1870, the population of the colony was less than 25,000 and all the British Government was prepared to allow the colonists was a Legislative Council of eighteen members, twelve of whom were to be elected and six nominated. That 1870 Legislative Council cannot be regarded as a truly democratic body because the elected members did not take their seats as a result of their election. After their election, they had to be formally appointed by the governor to be Members of the Legislative Council. The governor had the power to dissolve or prorogue the Council and the right to veto

44 Ogle, p282

any decision it made. Furthermore, the right to vote at elections was restricted to adult males who met the prescribed property qualifications. The Colonial Secretary, the Surveyor-General and the Attorney-General were members of the Council without the need to be elected.

The discovery of gold in the 1880s resulted in a dramatic increase in the population of the colony, and by 1887 it had risen to about 45,000 – not far short of the figure of 50,000 Nathaniel Ogle had claimed would qualify the colony for the right to frame its own constitution. In 1889, the Legislative Council passed a bill containing a proposed new constitution for Western Australia. Governor Broome then led a delegation to London to submit a petition asking for self-government under the constitution drafted by the Legislative Council.

That constitution was accepted by the British Parliament, but not without some debate. Some members of Parliament argued that the colony covered an area that was too large and believed that it should have been divided into two separate colonies with the boundary at Shark Bay. Other members were unhappy with the fact that the right to vote was, in the proposed constitution, restricted to men who owned or leased property. Broome and the delegation of prominent Western Australian citizens managed to persuade enough of the members of Parliament, and in 1890 Queen Victoria gave her assent to the establishment of the Colony's first responsible government.

Under the constitution granted to Western Australia in 1890 there was to be a Legislative Assembly of 30 elected representatives and a Legislative Council of 15 members appointed by the governor. In 1893, the population of the colony reached 60,000 and the constitution was amended to increase the size of the Legislative Council to 21 – three from each of seven provinces. It was also decreed that in future all members of the Council were to be elected. Western Australia's Government consisted entirely of elected representatives for the first time. However, the right to vote was still restricted to adult males who owned or leased property. It was not until 1899 that women were enfranchised.

Sir William Robinson, a former governor, was entrusted with the task of seeing the 1890 constitution implemented. He was unable to convince everyone in the colony that the constitution was exactly what was needed. For some, Section 70 was unacceptable. Under Section 70, an Aboriginal Protection Board under the control of the British Government was to be established, and £5,000 or 1% of the state's income – whichever was the greater – was each year to be set aside for aboriginal welfare. Broome did not expect the white settlers to deal fairly with the indigenous population, and the British Government decided to take his advice.

John Forrest, the state's first premier, disliked Section 70, but accepted the constitution as passed by the British Government in its entirety so that the colony could have its own government without further delay. Together with other like-minded members of Parliament, he acted to negate Section 70. In 1899, the Western Australian parliament passed a Constitution Amendment Act that repealed the Section and the Western Australian Government took upon itself the administration of aboriginal affairs. The obligation imposed by the 1890 constitution to set aside 1% of revenue for aboriginal welfare was subsequently ignored.

Under John Forrest's leadership and with money pouring into the Colony's coffers from gold mining, the fledgling government undertook an ambitious schedule of public works. About three million pounds was borrowed to finance the extension of the rail network into agricultural districts, timber areas and certain goldfields. Telegraph extension services and new public buildings were also constructed. The creation of a harbour at Fremantle and a pipeline to carry water to the Goldfields became projects and not just dreams. A lighthouse was also planned at Cape Leeuwin.

John Forrest was knighted for his services to the colony, becoming the first Western Australian to be so honoured.

The Western Australian constitution has been amended a number of times since it was first implemented. The number of electorates for the Legislative Assembly was increased to 50 in 1899, to 51 in 1968, to 55 in 1975 and to 57 in 1981. The Legislative Council had the number of its electoral provinces increased to 15 in 1963, to 16 in 1976 and to 17 in 1981.

**  **

While Western Australians were seeking the right to control their own affairs for the first time, politically-minded citizens in the other Australian colonies were advocating that their governments should surrender some of their independence in order to establish an Australian Commonwealth Government.

Sir Henry Parkes first proposed the formation of a Federal Council in 1867. When he became Premier of New South Wales he promoted the idea at a conference in 1880 at which representatives of Victoria, South Australia and New South Wales met to discuss matters that concerned all three colonies. The disadvantage of having completely independent colonies in Australia was perhaps most obvious in the different laws regarding imports in New South Wales and Victoria. Victoria had decided to protect local industries by taxing imported goods. There were no duties payable on goods imported into New South Wales. As a result, smuggling across the border from New South Wales to Victoria could be extremely profitable and it eroded the effect of Victoria's protectionist policies.

Queenslanders became more enthusiastic about Federation when the Germans and the French moved into New Guinea and New Hebrides; a united Australia would be more capable of preventing any European power claiming part of north Queensland. In 1883, the Premier of Queensland presented a draft federal constitution to delegates at a conference of representatives from all the self-governing Australian colonies and New Zealand. The conference endorsed the Queensland Premier's draft and the Imperial Parliament subsequently passed the Federal Council of Australasia Act, 1885.

That Federal Council did not accomplish much as the governments of New South Wales and New Zealand refused to take part in its deliberations or take notice of its decisions. At least it provided a forum where politicians could debate exactly how a true Australian Government should be constituted, and it was made clear that New Zealand was not going to surrender any part of its sovereignty to an Australasian Federal Government.

A number of meetings of representatives of the six Australian colonies were held in the next few years and they produced a draft federal constitution. In 1898 a referendum was held in New South Wales, Victoria, South Australia and Tasmania to allow the citizens to decide whether the constitution as drafted should be submitted to the Imperial Government. The referendum was unsuccessful because the majority required was not attained in New South Wales.

Another referendum was held the following year in every Colony except Western Australia. Voting in the 1899 referendum was 377,898 in favour of the establishment of a Commonwealth Government and 142,280 against it. Those promoting federation were in a strong position when they approached the Imperial Parliament to ask for the establishment of the Commonwealth of Australia.

The lack of enthusiasm for federation on the part the Government of Western Australia is not difficult to understand. During the 1890s, Western Australia was arguably the most prosperous of the Australian colonies. The mines at Kalgoorlie and Boulder were yielding a fortune in gold. Those who opposed federation could not see why the benefits of that new-found wealth should be shared with the other colonies. There was also a fear that the interests of Western Australia would not be protected in a federation because the state, with its small population, would have relatively few members in any House of Representatives. Furthermore, Perth's geographical remoteness and lack of rapid communication with the eastern states caused some Western Australians to become isolationists who developed a 'them and us' attitude.

There were three prominent Western Australians – John Forrest, James Lee Steere and J.W. Hackett – who were actively involved in the meetings of representatives of the six Australian Colonies at which federation was mooted. Alfred Deakin said of those three:

> *Sir John Forrest, and Dr J.W. Hackett were well-informed and capable members of the Convention, and with them was Sir James Lee Steere, a man of similar type and standing with the slowness of an Englishman uniting a very practical sense of all the issues involved and a kindness of disposition which made him a general favourite.*[45]

Of the three, only Forrest was inclined to be ambivalent about Western Australia surrendering part of its autonomy to a Commonwealth parliament. He attended the meetings and Deakin considered him to be *'well-informed and capable'*, but he was the Premier when Western Australia was the only Australian colony not to have a referendum regarding the proposed federation in 1898 and 1899.

Forrest was the premier of a colony riding on the crest of a wave of unprecedented prosperity he and his government were accomplishing great things. With C. Y. O'Connor

45 See the Journal of the Western Historical Society, December 1945, p15.

as his Engineer in Chief, a harbour had been created at the mouth of the Swan River and the pipeline from Mundaring to Kalgoorlie and the settlements in between was well on the way to being completed. There was far more prestige and satisfaction in being the premier of a thriving independent colony than just being the premier of a state in a federation. Forrest may also have been influenced by his brother Alexander who was an open and active opponent of Federation.

Alexander Forrest was a member of the Legislative Assembly and a leader among those who believed it was in Western Australia's best interests to remain independent. He campaigned around the Goldfields against Western Australia becoming part of the Commonwealth but failed to win a great deal of support for the anti-federation movement. A large proportion of the residents in the Goldfields had only recently arrived from the eastern states. When Forrest argued against the Colony becoming part of the Commonwealth, some migrants responded by advocating that the Goldfields should become a separate state and join the Commonwealth. They became known as 'Secessionists'. John Forrest and his government could not lightly dismiss the Secessionist Movement, because the colony would be in serious financial trouble without the wealth being produced in the Goldfields.

The Secessionists established a reform committee in London to lobby for the creation of a separate Goldfields state, and they sent a petition to the Queen requesting the formation of a new colony with its capital at Kalgoorlie. Secessionist rallies in mining towns managed to attract

good crowds. It may have been the activities of the
Secessionists – as well as the fact that there had been no
Western Australian referendum in 1898 or 1899 – that
prompted the British to omit Western Australia from the
Commonwealth that was created by the Constitution Bill
of July 1900.

John Forrest and his government became convinced
that a referendum was needed to decide the future of the
colony. There was no other way to end the debate between
the Secessionists, those who wanted all of Western
Australia to become part of the Commonwealth, and those
who wanted the colony to maintain its independence. The
referendum was held in July 1900 and the result was 44,800
for federation and only 19,691 against. This was the first
opportunity women had to vote in Western Australia.
The majority in favour of federation was overwhelming,
and feminists may like to contend that it was the votes of
sensible women that carried the day.

With the results of the referendum, Forrest applied to
the Federal Parliament for Western Australia to be included
in the Commonwealth. On 1 January 1901, the Chief
Justice of Western Australia addressed a rally on the Perth
Esplanade and announced that Western Australia would
be, from that day forward, a state of the Commonwealth
of Australia.

Chapter 15: *Iron Ore*

In 1880 iron ore was discovered on Koolan and Cockatoo Islands near Derby in the far north but at that time there was no reason to exploit the deposits. South Australia – almost as close to Perth as Derby – had vast deposits of iron ore on the Eyre Peninsular and a smelter that had been in operation since 1873. South Australia was the major source of iron for all of Australia until well into the twentieth century. Early attempts to establish smelters in New South Wales and Victoria had not been successful.

In 1899 Broken Hill Pty Ltd, a company that had been formed to mine silver, lead and zinc at Broken Hill, leased an iron ore deposit at Iron Knob and began shipping coal from Newcastle to Whyalla to fire its smelters there. In 1915 BHP fired up blast furnaces in Newcastle and its ships began sailing from Whyalla to Newcastle loaded with iron ore and back with coal. The First World War had forced Australia to become more reliant upon locally produced iron and steel.

During the period between the two World Wars the production of iron and steel in Australia became a major export industry. Much to the disappointment of the Trade Union Movement and the Labor Party, BHP sold a considerable amount of pig-iron to Japan in the 1930s. Trade unionists at the time feared the emerging power of the Japanese – the so-called 'yellow peril'. Prime Minister Robert Menzies was nicknamed 'Pig-iron Bob' by the unionists and subjected to a great deal of abuse for allowing the sale of iron to the Japanese who used it to equip their armed forces.

Critics of the policy of selling iron to Japan had good reason to be concerned. Japan had been Australia's ally during the First World War, but its leaders had begun to promote the idea of a Greater East Asia Co-Prosperity Sphere, a bloc of Asian nations led by Japan that would be free of domination by Western powers. A number of nations including Britain, France, Russia, Germany and America were occupying parts of Asia at the time. 'Asia for the Asians' was one of the lines Japan adopted to promote the concept of Asian Co-Prosperity while they prepared for war using Australian iron.

At the end of the Second World War the Western Australian Government decided that the state should begin producing its own iron. In 1945 a small charcoal-iron plant was established at Wundowie. The ore to feed the plant was mined at Koolan Island even though it was known that there was iron ore far closer to Perth in the Pilbara. The deposits in the Pilbara had been noted by a geologist, W.P. Woodward, in 1890, and the Goldsworthy ore body there had been discovered in 1938.

The Goldsworthy deposit was surveyed by the Mines Department in the 1950s, but it was not until some ten years later that anything was done to exploit the vast amount of iron ore in the Pilbara. It was Lang Hancock and Peter Wright who were responsible for that.

Hancock and Wright had been boarders together at Hale School and were close friends. Together they managed Mulga Downs Station during the 1930s. Hancock was managing the station on his own when, in 1952, he flew his light plane low over the Hamersley Ranges and either noticed the strange behaviour of his compass, or the rusty red walls of the gorge (both stories later gained currency). With the help of a prospector, Ken McCamey, he proceeded to investigate the extent of the iron ore deposits in the Hamersley area. They found vast bodies of iron ore; one of them became known as McCamey's Monster.

Hancock hoped to exploit the deposits he had discovered, but for a time the Commonwealth and State governments would not allow him to do so. The Commonwealth had placed an embargo on the export of iron ore to protect what it believed to be limited resources, and the State Government would not allow the pegging of claims over any iron ore deposits. After years of lobbying, Hancock was finally allowed to stake a claim in 1961. He then enlisted the help of his old friend Peter Wright to mine the ore body.

Meanwhile, Australia's relations with Japan had undergone a complete transformation since the time of the fear of the 'yellow peril'. Hatred for the Japanese, which had developed during the Second World War, had faded. Japan had recovered from the damage it had suffered during the war to the extent that it had had become one of Australia's best customers for primary produce. It had also become one of the world's leading industrial nations, but it was dependent upon imported raw materials. Japanese companies needed iron ore from Western Australia and this time there was no Australian campaign against the sale of pig iron.

The Commonwealth Government was persuaded to lift the embargo on the export of iron ore, and Hancock and Wright entered into an agreement with Rio Tinto, one of the world's largest mining companies, for the mining and the export of ore from their claim. Under the terms of the agreement, Hancock and Wright were to be paid royalties on every tonne of ore extracted from their claim. As a result, each of them was to receive something like $10 million per annum.

Hundreds of kilometres of railway lines had to be constructed for the transportation of ore from the inland mines to the ports of Dampier, Port Hedland and Cape Lambert. To attract people to live and work in the harsh climate of the North West, the mining companies offered generous rates of pay. Workers in their hundreds moved to the Pilbara and the population of the region increased an estimated ten-fold in ten years. New towns were established to house workers and their families, while the population of existing towns increased so much that demand for housing resulted in rent and house prices in the remote towns of Port Hedland

and Karratha becoming higher than those for similar properties in Perth.

The State Government, profiting from the royalties it was receiving from Rio Tinto, set about encouraging further exploration for iron ore and the development of new mines. Large deposits were discovered at Tom Price and Newman in 1969, at Pannawonica in 1972 and at Paraburdoo in 1973. BHP Billiton commenced operations at Mount Whaleback and proceeded to develop the largest single-pit open cut iron mine in the world – 5 kilometres long and nearly 1.5 kilometres wide.

Rio Tinto and BHP Billiton did not enjoy a duopoly over the extraction of iron ore in the Pilbara for long. Smaller companies such as Fortescue Metals, Atlas Iron and Moly Mines pegged claims over ore bodies. Fortescue, whose claims cover an area about the size of Switzerland, negotiated contracts to supply iron ore to China's burgeoning heavy industries. On the strength of contacts to supply the steel mills in China, Fortescue has become one of the world's largest traders of iron ore. In its first full year of operations it shipped more than 27 million tonnes of ore to China.[46]

The size and quality of the iron ore deposits in the Pilbara – which accounts for 95% of Australia's production of ore – tend to overshadow all other iron ore producing areas in Australia. However, there are other localities in Western Australia where valuable bodies of the ore have been found. At Koolanooka, inland from Dongara, mining of iron ore commenced in 1966, but the mine there could not compete with the Pilbara mining giants

46 The Fortescue Metals website www.fmgl.com.au Retrieved 25/01/2011

and it was closed down in 1972. In 2005 five companies, which had staked claims over promising ore bodies in the Murchison, agreed to form the Geraldton Iron Ore Alliance to promote the establishing of a viable mining business in the area. The Alliance hopes to make that area the second largest iron ore producer in Australia, and it claims that its members will be able to export a total of 60 to 90 million tonnes of ore each year.[47] The State and Commonwealth Governments have agreed to assist the development of mining in the area through the Oakajee Mid West Development Project. The State Government is planning a deep water port, an extended rail network to the mineral deposits in the Murchison and an industrial estate at a site close to Geraldton. The port and other facilities are scheduled to be operational in 2013-2014.[48]

About 50 kilometres north of Southern Cross there is an iron ore mine at Koolyanobbing, and 100 kilometres north of that there are mines at Windarling and Mount Jackson. A relatively small company, Portmans Iron Ore Limited, extracts ore from those mines and transports it to Esperance, and from there to China. The company also commenced mining on Cockatoo Island in 2002.

The prosperity of Western Australia has become so dependent upon on the export of iron ore to Asia that one cannot help but wonder what will happen when the supplies of the iron ore and of the other minerals mentioned in the previous chapter are exhausted. Mineral deposits are a finite resource. There are enough ghost towns surrounded by abandoned gold diggings in Western Australia to give cause to wonder.

47   www.gioa.com.au   Retrieved 25/01/2011
48   www.dsd.wa.gov.au/6616   Retrieved 15/01/2011

Chapter 16: *Petroleum*

The first recorded discovery of petroleum in Australia was made by Lieutenant John Stokes, an officer on *H M S Beagle*. The *Beagle* had returned Charles Darwin to England in 1836 at the end of a five-year circumnavigation of the globe and had then been assigned to serve as a survey ship with the Royal Navy. In 1839 it was being used in a survey of the Australian coastline from the Swan River northward. During the survey Stokes noted that there were traces of petroleum on the shore near North West Cape. The captain of the *Beagle*, John Wickham, named the inlet Port Darwin in honour of the famous passenger of their previous voyage.

Stokes' discovery of oil provoked little interest at the time. Until towards the end of the nineteenth century oil was recovered from the carcases of seals and whales. The reliance upon oil from animals ended when a way to refine kerosene from crude oil was discovered, extremely productive oil wells were drilled in America and petroleum began to dominate the world's markets for lubricants and fuel.

Around the beginning of the twentieth century a few wells were drilled in Australia in the hope of striking oil. There was some success when, near Roma on the Darling Downs in Queensland, gas was recovered and oil was extracted from shale. By 1906 natural gas was being used for lighting in Roma. During the Second World War, Roma's shale was a valuable – if limited – source of petrol because oil tankers from overseas were likely to be attacked by enemy submarines and raiders. Roma's gas was still being used for domestic purposes and power generation in southern Queensland in 2011.

In 1924, a well sunk near Lakes Entrance in Victoria yielded some oil, but not enough to be worthwhile exploiting.

After the Second World War, the Australian Government established the Bureau of Mineral Resources to collect data regarding the country's geology. The Bureau's data indicated that oil was most likely to be found in north-western Australia. Perhaps the discovery of oil by Lieutenant Stokes back in 1839 was noted by the officers of the Bureau.

Australia's first flowing oil well was drilled at Rough Range near North West Cape in 1952 by a company named Western Australia Petroleum – commonly called WAPET. For a time the well produced about 400 barrels of oil per day. Further wells were sunk, but it soon became clear that Rough Range did not contain a commercially viable oilfield. The company continued to explore, and in 1964 one of its wells struck a significant deposit of natural gas near Dongara. A pipeline was constructed to convey the gas to Perth, Kwinana and Pinjarra.

Geologists suspected that there might be petroleum deposits off-shore at Barrow Island and applied to drill there, but the Commonwealth Government restricted access to the area because the Montebello Islands (not far from Barrow Island) had been the site for testing atomic weapons between 1952 and 1956. Barrow Island had also been declared a nature reserve in order to protect its unique flora and fauna.

Eventually Western Australian Petroleum was permitted to drill for petroleum on the island subject to strict conditions to protect the environment. Exploration began there in 1964. Within a decade there were no less than 430 wells on the island and it had become Australia's most important source of oil and gas.

The North West Shelf – the continental shelf off the coast of Western Australia from the Pilbara up to Darwin – contains limited amounts of oil but it does hold vast quantities of gas. Japan and China were both eager to buy the gas, but conveying it to customers so far away posed problems. The solution was to liquefy the gas and transport it by ship. When liquefied its volume is reduced to almost one three hundredth of its natural size. Liquid natural gas (LNG) has become the third most important commodity produced in Western Australia, being surpassed only by iron ore and gold.

The importance of LNG exports to Australia's economy may be appreciated from the returns that are predicted will flow from just one project: the Gorgon Project. This project harvests gas from the Carnarvon Basin and processes it on Barrow Island. When fully operational, it is claimed, the Gorgon Project will lift Australia's annual gross domestic product by more than 60 billion dollars a year.[49] When the Wheatstone Project, planned to be based at Onslow, is also operational Western Australia will be second only to Qatar as a source of petroleum gas.

Australia's largest oil refinery, in Kwinana, was completed in 1955. It produces Liquid Petroleum Gas (LPG) and refines some oil from the Dongara field. Most petrol used in Australia is imported.

Yet to be exploited is the Browse Basin off-shore from Broome. It is considered to have the potential to be Australia's most important gas field. The State Government has plans for an LNG processing plant to be established on the coast not far from Broome. The Kimberley Land Council of the local aboriginal people approved of the development, seeing it as a valuable source of finance and employment, but there has been opposition from environmentalists and from some dissenting aboriginal people. At the time of writing the project was held up pending environmental approval from the Commonwealth Government and there were some unresolved legal actions.

There have been two major incidents in Western Australia's history of exploiting its reserves of oil and gas. In June 2008 a pipeline burst on Varanus Island off the Pilbara coast, the resulting explosion and a fire damaged the plant so seriously that it was three months before gas could again be piped to the mainland and six months before supply was back to normal. The State had become largely dependent upon petroleum gas for power generation and domestic use. The shutting down of the Varanus Island plant cut the supply of gas in Western Australia by a third, with serious consequences for the State's industries. Businesses were forced to reduce output and many had to cease operations. There were job losses and financial losses amounting to billions of dollars.

In August 2009 a leak developed at an oil rig on the Montana oilfield 630 kilometres off the Kimberley coast. Four attempts to plug the leak failed and oil continued to pour into the sea at a rate estimated to be as much as 2,000 barrels per day. During a fifth attempt the oil caught fire. The leak was stopped ten weeks later, but an oil slick drifted west over a vast area of the Indian Ocean, Timor Sea and Arafura Sea.

Chapter 17:

Western Australia At War

European settlement in Western Australia had always had a military presence. The colony at King George Sound in 1826 was at first a naval outpost to defend the western third of the island continent from any claim of sovereignty by France. The British Government then sent soldiers out to the Swan River settlement to protect the settlers from indigenous peoples. Western Australians have fought in many wars, including what some call 'the Aboriginal Wars' against Boers in South Africa; against Germans and Turks in the First World War; against Germans, Italians and Japanese in the Second World War; against North Koreans; against Communist Vietnamese; in Iraq and in Afghanistan. War memorials occupy pride of place in every significant town in the state. In King's Park the elaborate State War Memorial overlooks the City of Perth from Mount Eliza. It is one of many memorials and avenues of trees that honour those who died in battle and testify to the importance of Western Australia's military history.

The dawn service each Anzac Day at King's Park is always attended by thousands.

It is convenient to deal with Western Australia's military history in three sections.

First there was the undeclared, sporadic war between the colonists and aboriginal people which lasted for almost a century. Historians disagree about whether or not the fighting should be called a war. There was a period before Western Australia was granted its own responsible government and depended upon the British Army and Navy for defence, then came the pre-Federation period (1890 to 1901) when Western Australia had its own military force and its own government decided if and when its forces should go to war. Then after Federation defence became the responsibility of the Commonwealth Government and Western Australia was bound to abide by the decisions of the Commonwealth Government in all military matters and its citizens fought as members of the Australian Armed Forces.

THE 'ABORIGINAL WARS'

For the first few years of British settlement in Western Australia there was little trouble between the settlers and the aboriginal people. The colony at King George Sound in 1826 was small, and made no great claims over the areas in which aboriginal peoples lived and hunted. The settlement's commander, Major Lockyer, managed to establish a good relationship with the aboriginals by dealing effectively with the sealers who had abducted young native girls.

The arrival of hundreds of settlers at the Swan River settlement was bound to lead to trouble with the indigenous population. The settlers claimed title to land upon which aboriginals had been hunting and gathering for generations. The aboriginal people, having no appreciation of British laws regarding personal property and real estate, were liable to trespass, to kill and eat the settlers' animals. The settlers defended their legal rights. In the conflict that resulted aboriginals occasionally speared settlers and settlers responded with 'punishment raids' during which numbers of innocent aborigines were killed.

The number of British soldiers stationed in the colony was inadequate to provide security for all the settlers as they dispersed over a large part of the south west. It was largely left to the police and armed settlers to deal with indigenous militants such as Yagan, Calyute and their followers.

The indigenous population did not have the organisation, the numbers or the weapons to be able effectively to resist the European invasion. They could do no more than attack isolated individuals or small groups of explorers or settlers. The only major battle fought between the aboriginals and the Swan River colonists was the Battle of Pinjarra (briefly dealt with in Chapter 5) which was so one-sided that some historians argue that it should be called the Massacre of Pinjarra.

By the middle of the nineteenth century, the Aboriginal War in the Swan River area was virtually over. Foreign diseases, to which the Indigenous Australians had little resistance, played a large role in ensuring that the

Europeans prevailed. The settlers also had the advantages of having superior organization, horses and firearms.

Well after peace had been imposed upon the south west of the state, an undeclared war with the indigenous population continued in other areas of Western Australia. As explorers, settlers and miners ventured further into tribal lands they were often confronted with hostility from aboriginals who had no experience of dealing with the white men. In what has been called the frontier wars that followed there were a great many casualties on both sides, but the aboriginal population suffered the most by far. In 1868, for example, two policemen and two settlers were killed by a war party of the local Yaburara tribe near Roebourne. A posse of settlers set out in revenge, killing between 20 and 150 aboriginals. Estimates of the number killed varied widely.

The discovery of gold at Hall's Creek, which resulted in an invasion of hundreds of diggers into the tribal lands of the Djara, Konejandi and Walmadjari, also sparked a massacre of indigenous people. In 1887, some aboriginals were bold enough to attempt to protect their lands, but when John Durack was wounded by a spear, the diggers responded by hunting down and shooting a large number of them.

There was rarely trouble with aboriginal people on the goldfields. Prospectors descended on finds in such numbers that the indigenous population had little choice but to move away.

It was in the Kimberley that conflict between colonists and aboriginals resulted in the most serious toll of human life.

Between 1890 and 1920 the aboriginal population of the Kimberley was claimed to have been halved as settlers dealt with troublesome aboriginal peoples by shooting and poisoning them. Some historians refer to this period as the Killing Times.

The aboriginal people had their most redoubtable leader, a man called Jandamarra, during those years of conflict in the Kimberley. He led his people in a six-year campaign of resistance that was only ended when he was tracked down and shot by an aboriginal tracker working for the police.

Jandamarra became an outlaw when, after working with the police for some years he killed a policeman who had been his friend and set free a number of aboriginal prisoners. This rebellion he led became known as the Banuba War. He had the rifle that had been issued to him and the gun he had taken from the policeman he had killed. For the first time aboriginals were able to use guns against the colonials.

In 1894 Jandamarra led an attack against some drovers who were moving cattle to up a station on land traditionally occupied by the Banuba tribe. Two drovers were killed. The police responded by assembling a force of some thirty policemen and volunteers to hunt down Jandamarra and his followers. In Windjana Gorge Jandamarra was wounded but managed to escape while dozens of other aboriginals were shot and killed.

Jandamarra then proceeded to conduct a guerrilla campaign against the settlers in the Kimberley. He came to be regarded by the Kimberley people as having mystical powers.

When he was finally hunted down and shot by an aboriginal tracker with a modern rifle, his head was removed, preserved and sent to England as a trophy for the company that made the rifle that had been used to kill him. Jandamara's end was similar to that of Yagan in 1834.

The last shots were fired in the Aboriginal War as recently as 1926 in what has been called the Forrest River Massacre. At Forrest River, Reverend Ernest Gribble ran an Anglican Mission devoted to helping indigenous people. A pastoralist at a nearby station, Frederick Hay, assaulted aboriginal women, abducted one of them and inflicted grievous bodily harm upon an aboriginal man who attempted to defend the women. Gribble complained to the police about Hay's conduct and was told by the Protector of Aborigines, A.O.Neville, that he was just being an over-protective missionary.

Hay then raped a young aboriginal girl and horse-whipped an aboriginal man, Lumbia, who came to her aid. Lumbia killed Hay with a spear. Hay's badly decomposed body was found some weeks later, and a posse of about 14 armed men led by two constables assembled at Wyndham to hunt for the killer. They did not know who had speared Hay, so they arrested about 30 aboriginal men and took them in chains to Forrest River. In the course of making the arrests they shot and either killed or wounded dozens of other aboriginal people including women and children. The exact number of casualties is not known, but aboriginal record keepers numbered the deceased at about 100. Gribble put the number at about 30.

The slaughter was scandalous enough for the Western Australian Government to set up a Royal Commission to investigate. The commissioner recommended that the two constables be charged with the unlawful killings, but they never were. Lumbia was tried, convicted and sentenced to death, a punishment that was commuted to life imprisonment because he had been so seriously provoked.

After that incident the people and Government of Western Australia adopted a far more humane attitude towards aboriginal Australians. The Aboriginal War ended as it had begun with no formality such as a declaration of peace. It is not commemorated in the Australian War Memorial in Canberra and there are no memorials in Kings Park to those who died fighting. Some historians deny that there ever was such a thing as a war between settlers and indigenous Australians. Whether the conflict is to be called a 'war' depends on the definition of the term 'war', but there is no doubt that the years of conflict resulted in hundreds of casualties among the settlers and far, far more among the aboriginal people.

**  **

During the years that Western Australia was just a British colony without a responsible government of its own – 1826 to 1890 – British troops were involved in wars in New Zealand, Sudan, South Africa and China. If any Western Australians fought in those wars they would have done so as individual volunteers. There was no Western Australian military force. In 1885, only New South Wales sent a battalion of its own army to fight as part of the British forces in the Sudan.

THE PRE-FEDERATION PERIOD

After being granted responsible and representative government in 1890, Western Australia had to recruit its own defence forces and decide if its men should go to war.

During the Second Boer War the British Government asked each of the Australian colonies to provide troops. The New South Wales Lancers arrived in South Africa on 22 November 1899. A Western Australia contingent arrived at Cape Town four days later. They were combined with units from other states to form what was called the Australian Regiment. Western Australians played an important role in the relief of Mafeking and there were nine soldiers from the state involved in the defence of Elands River until the Boers withdrew.

Between November 1899 and May 1900, four contingents of between 110 and 150 volunteers sailed from Western Australia to fight in South Africa. Their names and some details of their service records are available through the Australian War Memorial and the Perth Dead Persons Society.[50]

AFTER FEDERATION

A further five contingents of Western Australians sailed for South Africa from Western Australia to fight the Boers between March 1901 and June 1902. They all enlisted as members of the Australian Commonwealth Horse Company. While there were Australians who distinguished

50 For further details consult the Dead Persons Society website at http://
www.perthdps.com/military

themselves in South Africa – six were awarded the Victoria Cross – the Boer War has not gone down in history as among Britain's finest victories.

It is estimated that about 16,000 Australians fought in the Second Boer War. Over 280 soldiers were killed in action or died from wounds inflicted in battle.[51] About 1,500 of the Australians who went to South Africa to fight were from Western Australia.

Within a decade of the end of the Second Boer War, Britain was preparing for the First World War. In 1914, Britain declared war on Germany, the Austro-Hungarian Empire and the Ottoman Empire. Australia, as a part of the British Empire, considered itself to be involved without any need for the Commonwealth Parliament to discuss the matter.

To help the mother country a volunteer force was recruited and named the Australian Imperial Force (A.I.F.). The ships to take the A.I.F. to Europe assembled in King George Sound in Western Australia, and departed for Europe in convoy on 1 November 1914. Near the Cocos Islands the escorting Royal Australian Navy's *HMAS Sydney* engaged in battle and sank the German cruiser *Emden*.

The Australian contingent was at first stationed in Egypt to defend the Suez Canal, and then men of the A.I.F. were sent with a contingent of New Zealanders to land at Gallipoli on 25 April 1915. In a fruitless and costly campaign intended to gain control of the narrow strait that provides access to the Black Sea, over 8,000 ANZACS were killed and more than three times that number were wounded before the troops were withdrawn.

---

51 See the Australian War Memorial website at http:// www.awm.gov.au/ atwar/boer.asp

Most of the remaining Australian soldiers were sent to fight in the trenches in France. The Light Horse units were directed to the campaign against the Turks in Sinai, Palestine and Syria.

Albany has always claimed a special link with the A.I.F. since it farewelled the convoy of Australia's first contingent of troops to the First World War. It also claims a special link with the Gallipoli campaign and with the Australian Light Horse. As well as a war memorial in the town, Albany has an impressive Desert Corps Memorial on Mount Clarence overlooking Princess Royal Harbour and King George Sound where the convoy assembled. Albany also claims to have held the first Anzac Day observance ceremony.[52]

Soon after the beginning of World War 1, Rottnest Island was taken over by the Commonwealth Government for the internment of enemy aliens and prisoners of war. The internees were German, Slav or Austrian men, most of whom had been working in mines on the Goldfields. By the end of 1915 about 1,000 internees were living on Rottnest, mainly accommodated in tents. Before the end of the war that camp was closed down and the internees were moved to Garden Island and Holdsworthy in New South Wales.

The First World War was fought a long way from Australia, but it did have a long-lasting effect on the national psyche. From a population of less than five million almost half a million young men enlisted to fight. Over 60,000 of them died in action and 156,000 were wounded or

52 See the South West Tourism Guide at http://www.discoverwest.com.au/albany.html
53 See the Australian War Memorial website at http://www.awm.gov.au/atwar/ww1.asp

gassed.[53] Anzac Day has become one of Australia's most important national days.

On 3 September 1939, Australia became involved in the Second World War when the prime minister asserted Australia's independence by making a declaration of war against Germany and Italy. No longer did Australia accept that it automatically had to be at war because Britain was at war.

Recruiting began for a volunteer force to fight overseas, and in Western Australia the 6th Division of the A.I.F. was formed. A major camp was developed at Northam, where up to 500 recruits at a time could be trained for service. New training bases were established at Cunderdin and Geraldton where aircrew could be prepared for service in the Royal Australian Air Force (R.A.A.F.).

On 20 January 1940 the 2nd A.I.F., which included the 6th Division, sailed from Fremantle to support the Allied forces in Europe and North Africa. They were accompanied by 3rd Squadron R.A.A.F. and a Brigade from New Zealand. A second convoy followed some three months later.

Steps were taken to defend Perth against a potential German attack. Gun emplacements were established on Rottnest and Garden Islands and heavy guns were placed on Buckland Hill, just north of Fremantle. In 1940, a Volunteer Defence Corps (V.D.C.) was established, drawing members principally from the ranks of those who had served in the First World War. This Australian version of Britain's Dad's Army eventually had over 43,000 members Australia wide. There were 11 V.D.C. units in Western Australian towns. As a division of the Australian

Army the V.D.C. had to be provided with uniforms and weapons from the Army's arsenal. The first rifles given to the V.D.C. were old relics of the Boer and First World Wars. Later more modern weapons were provided.

Once again 'enemy aliens' were imprisoned and Rottnest was used for an internment camp. This time, any men of German or Italian ancestry who were not able to claim Australian or British citizenship were arrested and imprisoned there. Women and children were regarded as no threat and were not interned.

Some of the 'enemy aliens' were conscripted to serve in the Civil Construction Corps. The 'C.C.C.' – unkindly called 'Curtin's Coward Corps' by some people – consisted of men who were not enlisted in the fighting forces. Men who were too old or unfit for military service or were 'conscientious objectors' and even some prisoners of war were compelled to work on the construction of airfields, roads and other infrastructure considered vital for the defence of the country. The Civil Construction Corps did some work upgrading the Eyre Highway because it was recognised as being important for national defence. They also constructed a number of airstrips in the tropical north of the state.

In November 1941, *HMAS Sydney*, the pride of the Royal Australian Navy, engaged a German raider, the *Kormoran*, in a fierce gun battle about 700 kilometres west of Geraldton. The *Sydney* was sunk and all of its crew – 645 men – perished. An impressive memorial now stands on Mount Scott in Geraldton, featuring a sculpture of 645 seagulls. The *Kormoran* also sank after the battle, but 340 of its crew of 393 were rescued. Just why the *Sydney* should have been sunk by a much smaller raider and why there were no survivors are questions that have never been satisfactorily answered, but in 2008 the wreck of the *Sydney* was located and some degree of closure has been accomplished.

With the benefit of hindsight, it is obvious that neither Germany nor Italy was ever likely to attack Australia. The Axis had more than enough on its hands in Europe and North Africa. However, a very real threat to Australia emerged suddenly, and largely unexpectedly, when Japanese aircraft attacked the American fleet moored in Pearl Harbour on 7 December 1941. John Curtin, the only Western Australian to be prime minister, defied Winston Churchill and brought the Australian Forces involved in fighting the Germans and Italians back home to defend Australia.

The Japanese army advanced through the Western Pacific and South-East Asia at an alarming speed. It conquered Malaya and then, on 15 February 1942, captured the great British fortress Singapore. Japanese aircraft sank the British battleships in the region and, for the first time in its history, Australia could no longer depend upon the protection of the Royal Navy. The Japanese then proceeded to conquer the Dutch East Indies until only the Timor Sea stood between Australia and the forces of Japan.

Conscription was introduced in 1942. Australia then had an army of volunteers (the A.I.F.) and another army of conscripts (the Citizens Military Forces) commonly referred to as the militia. The C.M.F. was at first intended to defend Australia against attack, but men of the militia were sent to New Guinea to attempt to stop the Japanese advance along the Kokoda Trail.

On 19 February 1942 Darwin was bombed by Japanese aircraft from the East Indies. Two hundred and forty Australians were killed. On 2 March the Japanese bombed Wyndham and much of the town was destroyed. Three weeks later Japanese bombers returned to destroy Wyndham's airstrip and set alight the town's fuel depot. The war had come to Western Australia.

The state prepared for air raids. Public air raid shelters were constructed in parks and individuals dug shelters in their own back yards. Strips of paper were glued to windows of houses and the plate glass display windows of shops were covered by planks to minimize the danger of flying glass if the area was bombed. Blackouts were practised with Air Raid Wardens ensuring that no lights were visible. When there was no blackout, there was brownout – no street lights, dimmed car headlights, and curtains drawn across windows. A Volunteer Air Observer Corps was formed to watch the skies around the clock and record all aircraft movements.

The War came even closer to Perth when, on the 3 March, Japanese aircraft struck at about 16 Allied flying boats that were at anchor in Broome harbour. The flying boats had arrived from the Dutch East Indies carrying refugees and some military personnel, and many of the passengers were sleeping on board when Japanese Zeros swept in from the sea. All the flying boats were destroyed by Japanese bombs and bullets. Almost 100 people were killed. The wreckage

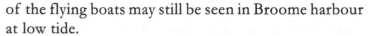

of the flying boats may still be seen in Broome harbour at low tide.

Derby was the next town to be subjected to an air raid, on 20 March 1942, but there were no casualties.

There were rumours that the Japanese would be landing, or had already landed, somewhere along the Kimberley coast, but there is no evidence that ever happened. A detachment of soldiers was sent to Broome, and smaller detachments were sent to other towns in the north of the state in case of invasion. Their purpose was to inform Army headquarters if any enemy troops landed rather than to repel the Japanese force. In case the Japanese decided to land on one of the beaches close to Perth, barbed wire was placed just above the high tide mark – with gaps so that people could swim.

Prime Minister John Curtin effected a major cultural change in Australia when, shortly after Japan entered the War, he appealed in the media to the United States of America to defend Australia, saying, 'Without any inhibitions of any kind, I make it quite clear that Australia looks to America free of any pangs as to our traditional links or kinship with the United Kingdom.'

Americans proceeded to arrive in Australia in their thousands, but not all Australians welcomed the presence of the 'Yanks'. There was a chauvinistic American song that began, 'Over there! Over there! Send the word, send the word to beware, for the Yanks are coming'. Some who resented the presence of so many Americans, along with their success in courting the local girls, claimed that the Yanks were not only over there, but also overpaid and oversexed. There were some major fights between Australian and American soldiers. In Brisbane shots were fired, about twenty men were seriously injured and one was killed. A brawl in Melbourne involved an estimated two thousand men and held up traffic in the central city area for an hour. There were other, less significant, fights in Newcastle and in Perth.

Fremantle became an important centre of military activity when the headquarters of the United States South-West Pacific naval force was established there and almost 20 American submarines began operating out of Fremantle Harbour.

A training base for the men in the Z Special Unit was set up on Garden Island. The men of that unit were trained to act as saboteurs, operating behind enemy lines. It became famous when the story of the raid by the *Krait* was told after the war.

The *Krait* was a Japanese boat that under the name *Kofuku Maru* had been owned by a Japanese fishing company based at Singapore. When Singapore seemed likely to fall to the Japanese William Reynolds used the boat to rescue evacuees. Reynolds and Captain Ivan Lyon of the Gordon Highlanders then together devised a plan to use the old wooden boat to strike a blow at the Japanese. Lyon convinced the Australian military that the plan was worth implementing, and the *Krait* was shipped from Colombo as deck cargo.

At the American naval base at Exmouth the *Krait* was made ready, and then fifteen men, four English and eleven Australians, went on board and set off for Singapore.

At Singapore harbour unchallenged the men of Z Special Unit set about attaching limpet mines to Japanese ships. Two of the ships were sunk and five were damaged, and the *Krait* safely returned to Exmouth. The Japanese believed that the explosions were the work of local saboteurs, and they arrested and tortured some residents in an attempt to find who was responsible. The Australian War Memorial acquired the *Krait* and it is part of the exhibition at the Australian National Maritime Museum.

A year after the *Krait's* successful raid, another group of commandos set out from Garden Island in a submarine on a similar raid, but after limited success they were killed by the Japanese.

The military adopted a policy of decentralisation and established supply depots and based small detachments in many country towns in the state. Other towns in the west received a boost when prisoner-of-war camps were established nearby. The population of the Dwellingup district was swelled by the arrival of no less than 1,500 Italian and German prisoners. Some of the prisoners were put to work on farms or in the timber industry and many remained in Australia after the War. There were no less than 28 places in Western Australia where prisoners of war camps were located.

The Second World War caused the Commonwealth Government to assume far greater control over the lives of Australians than it had ever exercised previously. It imposed the rationing of petrol, various food items and clothing. It even began to dictate fashions in clothing. Regulations provided that trousers for men must have narrow legs and no cuffs, and coats must be single-breasted and have no more than two buttons. For women the length and fullness of skirts was restricted and silk stockings were unobtainable. Newspapers were censored and the Jehovah's Witnesses were silenced. A 'Manpower Office' was established to decide who could work in what occupation. This office also had the right to move workers from 'non-essential' to 'essential' work. Wages and prices of goods were fixed by another Commonwealth Government bureaucracy.

When the War ended and there was no national emergency to justify the Federal Government exercising powers not granted to it by the Constitution, the Labor Government in Canberra organised a referendum hoping to amend the Constitution by giving it power to control wages and prices. The proposal was soundly defeated.

In 1951 the Commonwealth Government sent soldiers to fight in the Korea War in support on the United Nations Organisation. Any Western Australians who served in that war had voluntarily enlisted to be members in the A.I.F., R.A.A.F or the R.A.N. In view of what was seen as a Communist threat, the Commonwealth re-introduced conscription, but only for what was called 'National Service'. Conscripts were never sent overseas. Only males aged 18 were called up and were put through about six months of full-time training after which they had to continue as part-time members of the Citizen Military Force for a further five years. National Service was ended in 1959.

The United States of America was determined to halt the spread of Communism. By the Korean War it had prevented South Korea falling to the Communists. The next 'domino' it wanted to stop falling over (dominoes were the popular analogy of that time) was South Vietnam. By 1965, American armed forces had become involved in full-scale war against North Vietnam and the Communists in the south.

Australian Government became America's ally again. It introduced conscription in 1964, but this time, conscripts were liable to serve in Vietnam. For the first time a majority of the population disagreed with their country's involvement in a war. In 1969 a Gallop Poll revealed that 55% of participants wanted Australian troops to be brought home. The next year the Australian Government began a phased withdrawal of its forces from Vietnam.

In 1972 the Whitlam Labor Government was elected to take office in Canberra. One of its first acts was to end conscription. Australia's military involvement in Vietnam had begun in 1962 with a small group of 30 men and did not end until the Australian Embassy staff had been evacuated in 1975. It was the longest war in which Australia had ever been involved. About 60,000 Australian troops fought in Vietnam, and of those about 20,000 were conscripts. During the course of the war, 521 Australians were killed and over 3,000 were wounded.[54]

In Kings Park there is a Vietnam Memorial Pavilion where the names of 61 Western Australians who were killed fighting in the Vietnam War are engraved in a slab of black marble.

The sacrifice of Western Australian men in overseas military campaigns has continued unabated. There were

54   See 'The Vietnam War 1962-75' at Australian War Memorial at http://www.awm.gov.au/atwar/vietnam.asp

casualties when Australia aided the invasion of Iraq, in 2003. In 2011 the list of Australians killed in war was still growing. Two Australians have been awarded the Victoria Cross for their bravery in Afghanistan. One of them (Corporal Benjamin Roberts-Smith) is a Western Australian born in Perth and both were members of the Associates Rugby Union Club of Swanbourne.

Chapter 18: *A Bountiful Land*

In earlier chapters of this brief history Western Australia's shortage of water, harsh climate and poor soil were mentioned to explain why the Swan River Colony struggled to survive in its first few years. In fact, Western Australia always had the potential to be the most bountiful of the Australian states due to its mineral wealth and also its great capacity for growing of a wide range of food crops. With climatic conditions ranging from cool Mediterranean in the far south to the tropical heat of the far north, there are few plants that cannot be profitably cultivated in Western Australia, provided that they are given enough water and the deficiencies of the soil can be overcome.

Joseph Hardey, a settler who arrived in Fremantle in 1830 with a group of Methodist migrants, managed to farm profitably. Hardy persuaded Governor Stirling to grant to his party 512 acres some seven kilometres from Perth where the suburb of Maylands now stands. It was a peninsular of rich alluvial soil, and there the Methodist settlers succeeded in growing excellent crops of wheat, barley, oats and rye while other settlers around Perth were having difficulty growing anything.

The first wattle and daub cottage that Hardey built on the peninsular was swept away by a flood, as was the second His third residence, which came to be known as Tranby House, was constructed from mud brick and located on higher ground a safe distance from the river.

In 1967 the National Trust took action to prevent the demolition of the historically important farm buildings. It was too late to save the workers' cottage and the barn, but the Trust was able to take control of Tranby House and have it carefully restored. It is now one of Perth's tourist attractions.

Like the other early settlers, Hardey had at first attempted to recreate the type of farm he had known in England. He grew familiar crops and, when he realised that the climate of the Swan River area would allow the cultivation of plants that thrive around the Mediterranean, he also planted olive trees and grape vines. Being a strict Methodist, it is unlikely that Hardey would have fermented the juice from the grapes he had grown.

Following the pioneering work of Hardey and the others in the first generation of Western Australian farmers, a wide variety of produce has been grown in Western Australia.

GRAPES AND WINE

Grape vines were planted in Western Australia at Fremantle shortly after the first settlers arrived there in 1829. The first wine to be produced in the colony came from Olive Farm near Guildford in 1834, but growing grapes and making wine were not important activities in the nineteenth century in Western Australia. By 1895 only about 240 hectares were being used to grow grapes and wine production amounted to about 225,000 litres a year.[55] It was the sudden growth of the population due to the discovery of gold that increased the demand for wine, and by 1905 production was up to 837,000 litres a year.

After the First World War, land in the Swan Valley was sub-divided and allotted to returned servicemen. On their small holdings, many planted grape vines. Viniculture received a further boost between the Wars with the arrival of migrants from southern Europe – countries where wine production and consumption are part of the culture.

The Swan Valley was the dominant wine-producing area in the state until the second half of the twentieth century. Since then, it has been at least partially eclipsed by other areas that are producing highly regarded vintages.

The Great Southern Area – a vast belt that includes Albany, Denmark, Frankland River, Mount Barker and Porongurup – has become a major producer of good wines. George Egerton-Warburton, one of the pioneers of the Mount Barker area, planted grape vines there in 1859 and, a few years later, produced his first wine. Few other farmers in the area ventured into wine-making until an American Professor of Viniculture, Harold Olmo, spent some time in Western Australia and published a report in 1959, claiming that Mount Barker and Frankland were ideal for vineyards. Agricultural scientist Dr John Gladstones, an influential figure in the development of agriculture and

55 See 'Wine' at The State Library of Western Australia website at www.liswa. wa.gov.au/wepon/land/html/wine/hyml

viniculture in Western Australia, endorsed Olmo's opinion. More farmers then turned paddocks into vineyards and by the early 1970s the cool Great Southern district was producing a wide range of wine varieties that were regarded as superior to the products of the Swan Valley.

Dr Gladstones was also largely responsible for the development of what is now commonly regarded as the state's premier wine district – Margaret River. He investigated the suitability of the soil and climate of the region and published a favourable report in 1965. There are now dozens of wineries around Margaret River and the area has become noted for the fine wines it produces. Other vineyards have been established in the Blackwood Valley, the Geographe district, the Peel area in the Perth hills, and around Manjimup.

There are now over 400 vineyards in Western Australia from as far north as the Chapman Valley near Geraldton down to Albany.

CEREALS

Cereals have always been – and still are – Western Australia's most important crops. As mentioned in Chapter 5, Governor Stirling was mindful of the need for the colony to find areas more suitable for growing grain than the sandy coastal plain, so he established the Colony's first inland town at York in 1831. From York the area used for growing cereals has spread as far as the rainfall allows.

Growing cereals, although important for sustaining the population, was not a major source of income for the colony in the nineteenth century. It was an inefficient process involving manual planting and harvesting that was aided only by some horse-drawn machinery, and the crops were prone to disease (see Chapter 10). The farms were small by modern standards.

The introduction of steam-power tractors allowed farmers to clear land, plant and harvest faster and easier than ever before. Steam tractors moved slowly, but they were powerful. Not only were they used to haul agricultural implements, such as ploughs and harrows, they were also taken around to farms to be utilised as stationary power plants to drive threshing machines. The development of the internal combustion engine in the twentieth century ended the age of steam. An old steam tractor that was imported in 1889 has been preserved and now stands in the garden of the Gnowangerup Shire offices.

With the use of machinery – much of which came from America where the best methods of farming had been developed – the area under cultivation in Western Australia increased rapidly. The rust resistant wheat variety, 'Federation', and the network of railways constructed to service the mining industry were additional factors contributing to the rapid spread of farming in the Wheatbelt. From 1903 to 1913 the area under cultivation increased from about 100,000 acres to more than ten times that amount. An article in the New York Times on 7 January 1900 noted the increasing size of the Australian wheat crop and warned that the demand for American wheat products in Australia would decrease but that the demand for American agricultural machinery was increasing.[56]

---

56   See the New York Times January 7 1900 edition at http://query.nytimes. com/mem/archive-free.

From America came horse-pulled reapers and binders that enabled farmers to work more land without hiring more labour. The first Australian-made combine harvester – the Sunshine Harvester – was marketed in 1885. Combine harvesters were at first pulled by horses and then by tractors. The first Australian self-propelled combine harvester was the Sunshine Auto Header that came onto the market in 1923. With such machinery farmers in Western Australia were able to produce far more grain than was needed for domestic consumption and grain exports became an important element in the economy of the state. By the year 2000 roughly 4.5 million hectares were being sown with wheat each year in Western Australia – that is about 40% of the total area of Australia devoted to growing wheat. Over 90% of the wheat grown was being exported

There is no water available for irrigation in the Wheatbelt, so the success of the state's crops of wheat is completely dependent upon there being sufficient winter rain to load the soil with moisture prior to seeding. There were droughts in Western Australia in 1838 and 1877, but the first to seriously affect the production of wheat for export occurred in 1914. That year the grain yield was reduced by 80%. It became a common practice for farmers to turn sheep out to graze on fallow paddocks so that wool and meat could be a source of income in the drought years. There were further severe droughts between 1918-20, during the Second World War, and in 1967. Unless there is significant climate change, farmers in Western Australia will need to continue to profit sufficiently during good years to be able to remain on the land during droughts.

In order to avoid exhausting all the nutrients in the soil, nineteenth century farmers spread guano over their paddocks between crops. The supply of guano from islands off the Western Australian coast was seriously depleted by 1900 and virtually finished by 1904. Superphosphate then became the most commonly used fertiliser in the Wheatbelt.

An alternative to expensive fertilising was to rest a paddock for a year or two after it had produced a crop. The paddock would then be used for grazing sheep or growing something other than a cereal. Wheat and wool production tended to go hand in hand in the Wheatbelt and the planting of pulses in resting paddocks became a common practice.

Pulses are leguminous plants that improve the soil by adding nitrogen. Lupins and chickpeas are the two leguminous crops that have become most widely planted with clear benefits to wheat crops. The Department of Agriculture undertook a careful comparison of wheat crops grown continuously with the aid of fertilisers with crops grown in paddocks in which pulses were planted in rotation. Over a ten year period the average crop in the rotated paddocks was 1.75 tonnes per hectare while in the un-rotated paddocks it was 1.28 tonnes per hectare. The benefits of rotating crops instead of fertilising with chemicals were proved conclusively.

It was Dr John Gladstones who was to a large extent responsible for the successful introduction of lupins into agriculture in Australia. Working at the University of Western Australia and later at the Department of Agriculture, Dr Gladstones bred a number of varieties of narrow-leafed lupins suitable for growing in Australia. Those cultivars are now used throughout Australia, but some 80% of the lupin crops in Australia are grown in Western Australia.

However, it was not long until farmers began to find that wheat-lupin rotation inhibited the effectiveness of herbicides. Dr Gladstones produced cultivars of serradella – another legume – and it has proved to be particularly beneficial to areas of sandy, acid soils.

The formation of Co-operative Bulk Handling, established by the Wheat Board of Western Australia and Wesfarmers Limited in 1933, has proved to be a boon to farmers who no longer have to bag grain or individually sell their produce.

MARKET GARDENS

It seems that the early settlers were not particularly interested in market gardening. The journalist who wrote the article in the New York Times mentioned above reported that Australia was importing onions from America. Western Australia relied on imported potatoes, fruit and vegetables until the beginning of the twentieth century.

The growth in the state's population created by gold rushes drove a sellers' market for vegetables, and the authorities ensured there was suitable land available for market gardening. North of the Swan River was a chain of shallow lakes and swamps that were emptied.

Lakes and swamps at Osborne Park, Balcatta, Spearwood, North Perth, Bayswater, Midland and Bibra Lake were also drained, making acres of rich peaty soil available for exploitation. The flood plain at South Perth and Victoria Park was also turned over to market gardeners.

Many of those who took advantage of the reclaimed land were Chinese who had come to Australia hoping to make their fortunes from gold. The White Australia Policy caused a decline in the dominance of the Chinese in Western Australia's vegetable production. Between the two World Wars migrants from Italy and the Balkans arrived in Western Australia, taking over as the state's principal market gardeners.

By the use of fertilisers and regular watering from bores, the state's market gardeners are able to produce all the vegetables the population requires – although it is noticeable that some major supermarkets have recently taken to importing vegetables from China.

ORCHARDS

By the end of the nineteenth century apple, pear and citrus orchards had been established in the Swan Valley, in the Darling Range, at Harvey, Bindoon, New Norcia, Mount Barker, Katanning, and at the Blackwood River. Some small shipments of apples and oranges were sent to Britain as early as 1900, but it was not until cool storage was available on ships that orchardists could expect to do more than supply the local market. In 1910 the first commercial shipment of apples from Western Australia arrived in Britain in excellent condition as a result of cool storage. By the First World War, the annual shipment of apples from Western Australia to Britain had grown to be over 126,000 cases.[57] Packing sheds were established at Bridgetown and Mount Barker. Building the wooden cases in which the apples were packed also became a significant Western Australian industry.

By the use of fertilisers and watering throughout the hot dry summers, orchardists in the south west of Western Australia now grow – in addition to apples and pears – a wide variety of berries, citrus and stone fruits. The area has the advantage of isolation, so it has been comparatively free from the pests and diseases that cause losses to fruit-growers in other parts of the world. To maintain that advantage the state enforces strict quarantine regulations. The importation of fruit is controlled and people arriving in the state are compelled to surrender any fruit they may have with them. Despite those precautions, some of the worst pests have managed to arrive and establish themselves, in particular, the Mediterranean fruit fly, thrips, aphids and scales.

Tropical fruits are grown near Carnarvon, some 900 kilometres north of Perth close to the Tropic of Capricorn. In the 1920s Jack Buzolic planted some banana suckers beside the Gascoyne River. By 1930 he was selling bunches of bananas at the Perth Markets. There are now some 90 banana plantations at Carnarvon and a 10 metre high model of a banana has been erected at the corner of Robinson Street and Boundary Road to bring to the attention of visitors just how important banana growing has become to the town. Other tropical and sub-tropical

57 See The State Library of Western Australia website at http://www.liswa. wa.gov.au/wepon/land/orchards/html.

crops have been successfully grown in the area, including avocadoes, mangoes, paw paws, melons, pineapples, macadamia nuts and pecan nuts. The area also provides Perth with vegetables out of season.

The Gascoyne River provides the water that allows the cultivation of exotic plants near Carnarvon. It only flows on the surface for about a third of the year but, the water is always accessible by bore. In good years Carnarvon benefits from having a warm climate and plenty of water for irrigation, but the area is also prone to cyclones and torrential monsoon rain.

The Ord River scheme has provided the state with an alternative source of vegetables and tropical fruits. As mentioned in Chapter 14, Argyle Lake was formed by damming the Ord River in the early 1970s. It provides a vast volume of water for irrigation.

There were disappointing attempts to grow cotton, rice and sugar cane with water from Lake Argyle. Cotton proved to be an uneconomic crop because rampant weeds and destructive insect pests were almost impossible to contain even with the frequent spraying of herbicides and insecticides. Hopes have been recently raised of a resumption of cotton growing by switching from wet season production to dry season production and sowing genetically modified varieties of cotton that are resistant to attack by insects. Rice crops also failed and rice was last grown on a commercial scale in the Ord region in 1983.

In 2010, an attempt was made by two rice farmers from New South Wales to restart rice-growing using new varieties of seed. It remains to be seen whether this will resurrect commercial rice growing at the Ord. The world price of sugar fell so much shortly after the Ord scheme was under way that growing sugar cane there became unprofitable.

In recent years farmers in the Ord area have turned to supplying the Perth market with fruits that can be grown in the hot climate of the far north of the state, particularly melons and mangoes.

Chapter 19: *Tertiary Education*

Chapter 12 chronicled the steps taken in Western Australia towards the provision of a formal education for all children in the state. But as important as primary and secondary education may be, it is tertiary education that equips a society with the capability of advancement. Tertiary education in Western Australia owes much to John Winthrop Hackett, who played a major role in the foundation of the University of Western Australia.

Hackett was educated at Trinity College in Dublin where he graduated with a Master of Arts in 1874. For a short time he practised as a barrister, and then migrated to Australia. In Melbourne he became vice-principal of Trinity College and lectured in law, philosophy and politics. In surprising change of vocation, he moved to Western Australia in 1882 to manage a sheep station in the Gascoyne area. Within a year he had moved again - to Perth where, in partnership with Charles Harper, he became the owner and manager of the *West Australian* newspaper. In 1887, Hackett took on editorial responsibility. His editorials were often controversial, but through them he became influential in the politics of the colony. In 1890 the premier, John Forrest, nominated Hackett for a seat in the Legislative Council. It was a position he occupied until his death.

There have been few, if any, citizens in Western Australia's history who have been more involved in civic affairs than Hackett was. He and his newspaper were important supporters of C.Y. O'Connor (see Chapter 7). He was Diocesan Registrar and Chancellor of Saint George's Cathedral, chairman of the Kings Park Board and of the Karrakatta Cemetery Board, president of the Zoological Gardens Board and chairman of the Board of the Public Library. He was also largely responsible for the preservation of Queen's Gardens and Kings Park and for the establishment of the State Library, the Western Australian Museum and the Art Gallery.

Hackett regarded education as essential for improving Western Australian society. He served on the Board of Perth High School (later to become Hale School) for many years. Through the newspaper he campaigned for the establishment of a university in Perth, and in 1909, he was appointed to chair a Royal Commission set up to investigate the practicality of the state founding its own university. The Commission recommended that the University of Western Australia be established and, thanks to Hackett's casting vote, that there be no fees payable by the students.

In 1913 the University of Western Australia, housed in timber and corrugated iron buildings in Irwin Street, opened its doors to its first 184 students. Hackett was the founding Chancellor, and he personally endowed the chair of Agriculture.

There were – while the University was at Irwin Street – just three faculties: Engineering, Science and Arts. They provided courses to equip students to work in the state's principal industries – agriculture, mining and pastoral industries. There were also lectures in subjects such as the Classics, some modern foreign languages, and philosophy.

Hackett died in 1916. By his will he provided for his wife, son and four daughters, and then made bequests to many charities and public institutions. The Church of England received enough from the estate to build Saint George's College at the University. With Hackett's donation, the University was able to move to Crawley and erect the impressive Winthrop Hall and Hackett Hall on its new campus.

The move from Irwin Street to the site the University now occupies beside the river at Crawley was accomplished only gradually, and was finally completed in 1932. Many of the timber buildings from Irwin Street were transported to the new site, and one may still be seen at the University where it is used as the cricket pavilion.

By 1930 enrolments at the University had reached more than 600, but further growth was inhibited by the Great Depression. During the Second World War, the number of students entering tertiary study did not greatly increase. Young men were conscripted if they did not volunteer for military service, and young women were liable to be directed – at the discretion of the Manpower Office – to work that aided the War Effort.

The end of the War brought a sudden increase in the number of undergraduates. Returned servicemen were provided with substantial financial help if they chose to undertake a course at a University. Many enrolled, but a large proportion of them failed to adjust to normal student life and many did not finish their chosen course.

In the 1960s Western Australia's economy was boosted by the exploitation of the state's minerals. At the same time the children born in the post-War baby boom were reaching the age of matriculation. The value of a University degree was being increasingly recognised. By 1963 there were almost 4,000 students enrolled at the University of Western Australia and by 1975 the number of students had risen to over 10,000. The government then decided that the state needed a second university and planned to establish one at Bull Creek, south of the Swan River.

The new university was named Murdoch University, after Walter Murdoch – a popular academic, broadcaster and essayist who had begun lecturing at Irwin Street in 1913, and progressed to become the University's Chancellor from 1943 to 1948.

Murdoch University opened in 1975 with 510 students. In order to attract undergraduates it offered one course that the University at Crawley did not – Veterinary Science. It was also more flexible in its criteria for admissions, and claimed to be innovative in 'exploring new ways of thinking and making discoveries'.[58] In 2004 Murdoch University opened a Regional Campus at Rockingham, and in 2008 opened another at Mandurah. The University also established International Study Centres at Dubai and Singapore.

58   See the Murdoch University website at www.murdoch.edu.au/

By 2009 Murdoch University was catering for no less than 18,845 students.

In the 1980s the Director of Catholic Education in the Roman Catholic Archdiocese of Perth, Peter Tannock, was considering the establishment of a training college to provide teachers for the schools of the Diocese. Discussions within the Church resulted in a plan to establish a Roman Catholic University. With the support of the University of Notre Dame in America, a committee set about acquiring old and derelict buildings in Fremantle. The Barrack House Group provided most of the finance, but it became insolvent in the mid-1990s and for a time it seemed that the University of Notre Dame in Fremantle might never become a reality. An appeal for funds within the Church allowed the renovation of the buildings to proceed and in 1992 the first 70 students were admitted.

With financial support from the Federal Government, the University of Notre Dame in Fremantle grew rapidly. Its facilities were expanded to the extent that it could cater for up to 6,000 students. Notre Dame opened a branch in Broome and a Sydney campus in 2003. The Sydney campus caters for almost 2,000 students. In 2004 Notre Dame took the bold step of establishing its own School of Medicine.

Those three Universities have not been the only institutions providing tertiary education for Western Australians. There were, from early in the twentieth century, vocational colleges where people were equipped for employment in occupations that required training but not a university degree. Perth Technical College took in its first students in 1900. A Teachers' Training College was established at Claremont in 1902, and the School of Mines was opened in Kalgoorlie the same year. Muresk Agricultural College was opened in 1926 and a School of Physiotherapy and Occupational Therapy welcomed its first students in 1950. A second Teachers' Training College was opened at Graylands in 1955.

As the state's population continued to grow, other institutions were established to train the school teachers for the state education system – the Western Australian Secondary Teachers' College, Nedlands College of Advanced Education, Mount Lawley Teachers' College and Churchlands Teachers' College.

In the 1980s, Western Australian educational authorities decided to combine all the vocational colleges to form just two major technical schools – one based north of the Swan River and the other to the south. Eventually, this led to the creation of two more universities in Western Australia.

The teachers' training colleges were brought together under the name: The Western Australian College of Advanced Education. In 1991, the combined colleges were granted the status of a university and renamed The Edith Cowan University (Edith Cowan was the first woman to be elected a member of the Western Australian Parliament). The University now caters for about 20,000 students. The state's School of Nursing that provides nurses with a University Degree – something nurses had long been campaigning for – and the Western Australian Academy of Performing Arts are both departments of

Edith Cowan University. It also offers courses in Business, Law, Computing and Education.

The Perth Technical College, the School of Mines, the Muresk Agricultural College and the Schools of Physiotherapy and Occupational Therapy were brought together under the name of The Western Australian Institute of Technology. In 1986 it changed its name to 'The Curtin University of Technology' to honour John Curtin (the only Western Australian to occupy the office of prime minister). In 2010, the reference to technology was dropped. It has become the largest of the state's tertiary education institutions with about 44,000 undergraduates scattered over several campuses including regional and interstate.

Curtin University has made a serious effort to cater for minority ethnic groups, including indigenous Australians. It claims to have the largest number of aboriginal students of any university in Australia, and it boasts a Centre for Aboriginal Studies that, according to the University's website, 'aspires to contribute to positive social change for indigenous Australians through higher education and research.'

Chapter 20: *Multiculturalism*

This brief history began with dark-skinned hunter-gatherers as the only humans in Western Australia until the British arrived. For a short time, the people of Western Australia were either British or Australian aboriginals, but it was not long until the races were mixed. 'Half castes', as individuals of mixed races were called, posed a problem for the Colonial administrators in the nineteenth century.

That issue was addressed by the Legislative Council in 1886, when, under the leadership of Governor Broome, it passed the Aborigines Protection Act. That act was commonly called the 'Half Caste Act' because it stated that 'half castes' living in indigenous communities should be regarded as aborigines.

Prior to the 1886 act there was no law to protect aboriginal peoples from exploitation by the white settlers. The 1886 act may not have done a great deal to improve the way indigenous Australians were treated, but at least it ensured that settlers employing aboriginals had to provide them with 'substantial good and sufficient rations', blankets and clothing. The Legislative Council also set up an Aboriginal Protection Board and decreed that aborigines must be allowed to continue to hunt in areas where they traditionally did so.

That Aboriginal Protection Board did not last for long. In 1890 the British Government granted the colony self-government and inserted a provision (-Section 70-) in Western Australia's first constitution providing for the establishment of an Aboriginal Protection Board under the control of the British Government. That Board was also soon consigned to history. The new Western Australian Government had Section 70 repealed and proceeded to ignore the obligation that had been imposed by the constitution to set aside 5,000 pounds per annum or 1% of the colony's income each year for aboriginal welfare.

When the six Australian colonies were deciding what powers to confer upon the Federal Government they chose not to hand over responsibility for aboriginal affairs. By Section 51 of its constitution the Commonwealth Government was given power to make laws 'for the peace, order and good government of the Commonwealth with respect to ...the people of any race other than the aboriginal race.'

Left to deal with the problem of aboriginal welfare in its own way, the Western Australian parliament passed the Aborigines Act in 1905. The act stated that that the Chief Protector was the legal guardian of every aboriginal and 'half caste' child until they reached the age of 16. For better or for worse, the Chief Protector separated children from their mothers and placed them in institutions so that they might receive some formal education. Culturally insensitive he may have been, but the Chief Protector was acting *in loco parentis*. It was the accepted practice in England at the time for the sons of the wealthy to be packed off to boarding school at a young age. Life in the mission schools may not have been any worse than life in England's boarding schools as portrayed in Thomas Hughes' classical 1857 novel *'Tom Brown's Schooldays'*.

Condemnation of the policy came to a head in 1997 when the Human Rights and Equal Opportunities Commission set up an enquiry into the consequences of separating children from their aboriginal mothers. Under the chairmanship of Sir Ronald Wilson the evidence of hundreds who had endured that separation was received and a report entitled *'Bringing Them Home'* was published. Since then there have been public apologies by Commonwealth and State governments, 'Sorry Days' and claims for monetary compensation.

Long before the Human Rights and Equal Opportunity Commission's enquiry the Western Australian government had been gradually amending its policies regarding the aboriginals and 'half castes'. The era of stolen generations was effectually ended in 1963 when the Chief Protector lost the power to take aboriginal and 'half caste' children from their parents. Since then, children of all ethnic origins in Western Australia have come under the protection of the Child Welfare authorities.

* *  * *

The discovery of gold brought a great many non-British immigrants to Australia, further complicating race relations. Some of those immigrants fitted easily into the predominantly British society of the period. Some, like the Chinese, did not.

The Federal Government was granted responsibility for immigration policy under the Commonwealth Constitution. As one of its first pieces of legislation, the newly established Australian parliament passed the Immigration Restriction Act of 1901 by which immigration was restricted to the British and other Europeans who could be expected to fit in to the Commonwealth's British society. The attempt to keep Australia predominantly British became known as the 'White Australia' Policy. The policy was maintained until the end of the Second World War. John Curtin expressed the hopes of many Australians when he said, faced by the threat of a Japanese invasion, 'This country shall remain forever the home of the descendants of those people who came here in peace in order to establish in the South Seas an outpost of the British race.'[59]

The White Australia Policy is now condemned by many people, but it was widely supported when it was created. The policy's strongest support base was the working class, who did not want their chances of striking gold or finding employment being taken by foreigners – particularly by Chinese in the Goldfields and South Sea Islanders in the cane fields.

With a selective immigration policy, the Government had to give its immigration officers some legal way to keep

59 See the Australian Government Department of Immigration and Citizenship website at www.immi.gov.au

out people of the 'wrong type'. One method used was the dictation test. Those seeking to enter Australia could be ordered to take a spelling and dictation test. If they failed they could be refused admission. The regulations regarding the test did not specify in what language the test should be.

The Second World War shifted the perspective on the White Australia Policy. The Commonwealth began to realise that Australia, with its small population spread over such a large continent, was vulnerable to invasion. The Commonwealth Government, without holding a plebiscite to test public opinion or consulting state governments, decided to adopt a 'Populate or Perish' policy. It proceeded to exercise the power granted in Section 51 of the Commonwealth Constitution to legislate regarding 'naturalisation and aliens'. Migrants from Britain and from Europe were actively encouraged and even assisted financially to come to immigrate to Australia. Large numbers – particularly from Britain and from Italy, Greece and Yugoslavia – took advantage of the opportunity to make a fresh start after the traumatic experiences of the War.

The immigration of non-Europeans was discouraged, but gradually the White Australia Policy was eroded. In 1947 the Commonwealth government relaxed the policy a little by allowing non-Europeans to settle permanently in Australia to run businesses and so help the country's economy. The Colombo Plan in 1950 then opened the door to Asian students. The tertiary education industry has profited from the fees paid by overseas students ever since. The dictation test was abolished in 1958 and the next year the sponsoring of Asian spouses for Australian citizenship was allowed. The Whitlam Labor government finally ended the White Australia Policy by passing the Racial Discrimination Act of 1975, making race illegal as a criterion in any official dealings.

Since 1975 Australians have had to accept that the country is becoming home to an increasing number of immigrants of different races with different languages and cultures. According to the Immigration Department, Australia's population in 2010 was over 22 million. More than a quarter of the population were immigrants, and about 200 different languages were being used in Australia. The 2006 Census had found that 45% of Australia's population were either born overseas or had at least one parent born overseas.

It is now Commonwealth Government policy to consider the cultural differences of migrants to be desirable. Multiculturalism has become the politically correct ideal. The concept of Australia being 'in the South Seas an outpost of the British race' has been consigned to history.

How long multiculturalism will last in Australia time will tell. Cultures are not permanent. Customs, language, dress, technology and social structures change. In Western Australia indigenous peoples have almost completely given up the old 'hunter-gatherer' lifestyle and have either found employment or are living on the social welfare handouts. For all Australians the culture of their parents and grandparents is constantly being eroded by the influences of modern technology and the way it brings ideas and trends from overseas — uncensored — into Australian homes.

Ethnicity has rarely been a constant in the history of humanity. Races sharing the same geographical area tend to coalesce. One has only to consider the history of England where Celt, Roman, Angle, Saxon, Jute, Viking and Norman genes have been combined to produce the modern English people. Following that pattern, ethnic differences within the Australian population will probably diminish with time.

The Australian Government is doing something to preserve the existing Australian culture. It finances the Australian Broadcasting Commission and has legislated to enforce the airing of Australian programmes on commercial television for a certain percentage of the time. In support of multiculturalism it also finances S.B.S. – a multicultural telecaster.

One thing is clear: the days of Australia existing as an 'outpost of the British race' are over. The beginning of the end was made clear when the legal ties that bound Australians to the 'Old Country' were cut in 1971. Since then, Australians have not been entitled to British passports and are classified as foreigners by British immigration officials.

The states of Australia are gradually losing the characteristics that once distinguished them. Migrating interstate in the course of employment is now commonplace. The education systems of the states are being standardised so that children have fewer problems moving from a school in one state to a school in another. The laws of the states are increasingly being superseded by Commonwealth laws or amended so that differences between the laws of

all states are diminishing. Soon, there may be very little
modern history of Western Australia – distinct from the
history of Australia – worth writing about.

Chapter 21: *WA Inc*

In the 1980s Western Australia enjoyed the benefits that flowed from the exploitation of its deposits of iron ore and petroleum. The population of Perth was growing at an unprecedented rate. For shrewd businessmen it was an age of opportunity.

The extent of the involvement of the Western Australian Government in the dubious dealings of a few entrepreneurs was eventually revealed when a Royal Commission in 1991 investigated what became known as WA Inc. As a result of that investigation a number of people were charged and found guilty of criminal activity. The collapse of the companies set up by the entrepreneurs cost the state, the banks and small investors millions of dollars.

The principal individuals involved in the dealings of WA Inc were: Brian Burke, then premier; Julian Grill, Industrial Development Minister; and businessmen Alan Bond, Laurie Connell, Warren Anderson and Dallas Dempster.

Alan Bond, who was originally a sign writer, went into the business of land speculation. He bought land using borrowed money, subdivided it and sold it at a profit. Recognising that it would be in his interests to have friends in positions of power, he gave financial support to the State Labor Party. Laurie Connell and Dallas Dempster did the same. The state government, led by Brian Burke, then quite wrongfully provided financial backing for Bond's and Connell's commercial deals. Before long Alan Bond was being hailed by some journalists as Australia's wealthiest man. They cannot have taken into account that his assets – while they were, for a time, considerable – probably never did amount to more than his liabilities. He was freely spending money borrowed on the security of assets the valuation of which could be said to have been at least optimistic if not fraudulent.

Living like a millionaire, Bond set out to win the America's Cup. In that he succeeded, and Prime Minister Bob Hawke celebrated the victory as though it were a great triumph for Australia. The Americans then had to come to Fremantle to win the Cup back. Bond managed somehow to have the City of Stirling depart from its own building regulations and allow him to erect the only multi-storied building at Scarborough Beach – the hotel he named 'Observation City' – from which guests could watch the America's Cup defence.

Faced with a constant problem of having to find money to keep his creditors at bay, Bond purchased a controlling interest in a well-established Western Australian company with substantial assets that happened to be experiencing a cash-flow problem – Bell Resources Limited. Cash to pay for that deal was advanced to Bond by the Government

Employees Superannuation Fund. Bond then proceeded to strip Bell Resources of all its assets in order to keep Bond Corporation afloat. An estimated $800 million was siphoned off and Bell Resources became an empty shell. Scores of people in Perth, who had invested in shares in what had been one of the state's most solid companies, suddenly found that their shares were worthless.

Laurie Connell, best known for his involvement in horse racing and for a twelve-month prison sentence he served for race-fixing, established Rothwells Merchant Bank. When Rothwells ran into financial trouble in 1987, Premier Burke arranged for the government to provide a guarantee for Rothwells in an amount of $150 million. The government rescued Connell's company three times. Burke was probably willing to help because he had been involved with Connell in arranging for the state government to buy Northern Mining from Bond for millions of dollars over a fair price.

In 1986 a government agency – the WA Development Corporation – sold a large part of a block on the southern side of Saint George's Terrace to the Bond Corporation and the State Government Superannuation Board for a bargain price. Two years later the site was sold and Bond Corporation reaped a profit of millions of dollars.

Connell, in a joint venture with Dallas Dempster, paid a deposit of $100,000 on land at Kwinana. They claimed they intended to establish a petrochemical plant there. Western Australian Government Holdings poured about $170 million into the planning of the plant and paid Bond Corporation substantial 'management fees'. The land remained undeveloped and was eventually sold for $400 million, giving Connell and Dempster a huge profit.

Bond Corporation continued to grow with borrowed money and the support and financial backing of the state government. It erected the tallest building in Perth on the corner of Saint George's Terrace and William Street, and its offices in the top floors of the tower housed some notable works of art – including Van Gough's $54 million 'Irises'. It went into the beer and hotel business and for a time controlled a large share of Australia's breweries. It even made an unsuccessful attempt to gain control of Britain's largest brewery, Allied Lyons. There seemed to be no type of enterprise in which Bond Corporation would not be interested if there was a chance that money was to be made. It purchased Channel Nine from Kerry Packer. Packer famously observed that a person like Bond does not come along very often and when he does you have to take advantage of him. Within a short time Packer was buying Channel Nine back from Bond at a price many millions of dollars less than the price at which he had sold it to him.

The share market collapse in 1987 brought down the house of cards of WA Inc that Bond and Connell had constructed. The State Government's guarantees were not enough to save Rothwells. It was wound up and its creditors were paid in part with funds from the state government that it had to provide as guarantor. Bond Corporation's creditors demanded payment and Bond could not find the money to pay them. Faced with the probability of the revelation of his part in the dealings of Bond and Connell, Burke resigned from Parliament in 1988 and was succeeded as Premier by Peter Dowding.

Despite the rumours about WA Inc, the Labor Party managed to win power again at the next state election in 1989. Due to his links with Burke and WA Inc, Dowding was pushed into resigning as Premier in February 1990. Carmen Lawrence became the first woman to be a state premier in Australia.

Carmen Lawrence announced that a Royal Commission would be established in order to hold culprits answerable for the WA Inc scandal. That Commission took evidence over a period of 21 months. Its findings fill no less than six volumes and cover, in addition to those matters mentioned above, a number of other dealings made by the State Government that were not in the public interest.

Much of the money that had passed through the accounts of Bond Corporation could not be traced or recovered. Bond was subject to an intense examination in court, but claimed to be unwell and to have suddenly lost his memory. He was declared bankrupt, but he and his family somehow continued to enjoy the life of the rich. Very little of the money the state government had directed to supporting Bond and Connell has been recovered.

Bond, Connell and Burke were all convicted and served time in prison.

Chapter 22: *Wrongful Convictions*

WA Inc was a most serious example of official corruption, but it was not the only case of maladministration in the history of Western Australia. The conduct of a number of members of the Western Australian Police Force and the State Department of Public Prosecutions was found to be reprehensible in four widely publicised cases in the latter half of the twentieth century. No official inquiry or Royal Commission into those matters has ever been held in Western Australia.

In 1963, Eric Edgar Cooke was convicted on a charge of murder and sentenced to hang. Once convicted he freely admitted to something like 250 burglaries, 22 violent crimes, 8 murders and 14 attempted murders. Although he swore on a Bible that he had killed Rosemary Anderson and Jillian Brewer, the police and the Department of Public Prosecutions chose to disregard his confessions. They were satisfied that they had solved both those crimes. Cooke was executed by hanging. He was the last person to suffer that fate in Western Australia.

In 1963 John Button had been convicted of the manslaughter of Rosemary Anderson by vehicle impact. It was alleged that he had deliberately run down his girlfriend, Rosemary Anderson, when she had decided to walk home alone after an argument. He was questioned by the police, and did not create a good impression because he was a serious stutterer. After some 22 hours of interrogation during which he claims he was beaten, Button –according to the police –confessed. He pleaded not guilty, but the evidence of the police was believed by the jury and he was convicted and served five years of a prison sentence before being released on parole.

Button attempted to clear his name in a number of failed appeals to the courts and for ministerial intervention. The Court of Criminal Appeal finally overturned his conviction in 2002. Expert evidence established that his small car could not have been the one that ran down Rosemary Anderson but that the type of car that Cooke drove could have. Button was given an ex gratia payment of $460,000 by the State Government.

Darryl Beamish was a deaf mute and was just 18 years old when Jillian Brewer's body was found. She had been brutally killed with a tomahawk and dressmaking scissors. On the evidence of what was alleged by the prosecution to be a detailed confession freely given to the police, Beamish was convicted and sentenced to death by hanging in 1961. His sentence was commuted to life imprisonment and he was released after spending 15 years in prison. In 2005, Beamish's conviction was overturned, though he had to wait until June 2011 to be paid compensation for his wrongful conviction. For the 15 years he had spent in prison the State Government agreed to give him just $425,000.

In both cases the judges in the Courts of Criminal Appeal concluded that the confessions that led the juries to return a guilty verdict should not have been accepted as genuine admission of guilt. Cooke's freely-given confession to both crimes was accepted as most likely to be the truth.

It may be that in both cases the police had honestly believed they had arrested the right man. They had set out to obtain convictions and had been prepared to bend the rules to accomplish that.

At the time Beamish and Button were charged, interviews of the accused by the police were not required to be video-recorded. There were no CCTV cameras in police stations to film how prisoners were being treated. It was therefore easy for police to type or write out a convincing confession and then swear in court that it was an accurate record of what the accused had said in an interview. That practice was known as 'verballing'. Juries could be faced with two or three police officers, practised and plausible witnesses, claiming that their record was true. If a far less plausible prisoner denied that he had said what the prosecution alleged, a jury understandably would be inclined to accept the evidence of the police.

A further notable case of a wrongful conviction occurred in 1982 - that of the Mickelberg brothers. Three couriers collected $600,000 worth of gold from the Perth Mint and paid for it with worthless cheques.

Detective Sergeant Don Hancock, who had a reputation for nailing criminals, was put in charge of the investigation. He became convinced that the three Mickelberg brothers – Ray, Brian and Peter – had taken the gold.

There were reasons why he suspected the Mickelberg brothers were involved in the heist. They had been involved in the sale of a manufactured gold nugget to Alan Bond for far more than it was worth. Furthermore, the gold taken from the Mint had been traced as far as Jandakot Airport where Brian Mickelberg was a pilot.

Hancock arrested Peter Mickelberg, the youngest of the three brothers, and with Detective Tony Lewandowski allegedly took notes of what Peter confessed. The unsigned confession was later produced at the trial of the Mickelberg brothers and all three were convicted. They were given harsh sentences for a crime that had involved no violence – 20 years for Ray and 12 for Peter

Brian's conviction was overturned but he was killed shortly afterwards when the aircraft he was flying crashed. Ray and Peter Mickelberg maintained their innocence, and for years after they were released they fought to clear their names. Seven appeals by the Mickelbergs to the Court of Criminal Appeal were unsuccessful and then they were suddenly vindicated.

Don Hancock retired and moved to a small mining town, Ora Banda, to run the hotel there with his daughter helping as the barmaid. In the year 2000 a group of Gypsy Jokers – a notorious 'bikie' gang – arrived at Hancock's bar and abused his daughter. He ejected them from the bar, and they went off to a campsite. During the night a shot was fired and one of the Gypsy Jokers was killed. The other Gypsy Jokers considered that Hancock was responsible for the shooting. Shortly afterwards the Ora Banda hotel was destroyed by fire.

Hancock returned to Perth. One Saturday he and a friend went to the races together. As they drove home the car in which they were travelling was destroyed by a bomb and they were both killed.

Tony Lewendowski decided that he needed to clear his conscience. He admitted that the confession that had ensured the conviction of the Mickelbergs had been fabricated. Ray and Peter Mickelberg demanded compensation and an apology. Their demands were met with a payout, the terms of which were never revealed, and a public apology from the Western Australian Police.

The fourth notable case of a miscarriage of justice concerned Andrew Mallard who – like Button and Beamish – had a disability.

Andrew Mallard suffered from a bi-polar disorder, was unemployed, had low self-esteem and smoked marijuana. He was known to the police, and he lived just a short distance from a jewellery shop owned and run by Pamela Lawrence in Mosman Park.

On 23 May 1994, Ms Lawrence was brutally murdered in her shop. The police spoke with Mallard regarding the murder on a number of occasions – a few times when he was in the psychiatric hospital – but they only recorded what they claimed he admitted during their last eleven-hour interview. He was charged with the murder, and at his trial the prosecution relied to a large extent on police notes of what was claimed he said during those eleven hours and a video recording of about twenty minutes towards the end of that interview. That Mallard spoke of the murderer in the third person, that at times he seemed to be just speculating as to how the crime might have been committed and that he did say some very strange things did not, the prosecution maintained, mean that he had not confessed to murdering Ms Lawrence. No DNA evidence was offered and no murder weapon was produced. No allegation was made that Mallard had any of the victim's blood on his clothes or on his person even though it had been a particularly bloody murder. The explanation offered for the lack of blood was that Mallard had gone down to the river and immersed himself — clothes and all — in the water there. Mallard was found guilty, sentenced to life imprisonment and served twelve years in prison before being released on parole.

An appeal by Mallard against his conviction was heard by the Court of Criminal Appeal and later the High Court. The judges of the High Court were extremely critical of the way the police and the prosecutors had approached the prosecution of Mallard. Police and prosecutors are supposed to investigate a crime in a neutral way, to reveal to the defence all the relevant evidence, and to ensure that the court is presented with all the facts so that justice will be done. That was certainly not done in the Mallard case. Evidence that seemed to help Mallard was not revealed to his counsel or to the court at the trial. There had been a palm print on Ms Lawrence's counter from the hand of Simon Rochford who was later convicted on a charge of murdering his girlfriend with a weapon that could well have been the one that killed Ms Lawrence. That was not revealed to the defence nor was it investigated by the police at the time. The police had obtained a written report from an expert on the effect of immersing clothing in river water. A copy was provided to the defence, but only after two pages had been removed in which the expert stated that salts from the river water would have remained in the clothes unless they were subsequently thoroughly washed in fresh water. A witness gave a statement to police and provided a sketch of a man – not at all like Mallard – she had seen enter the shop at about the time of the murder. In her statement she referred to her drawing. The copy of her statement given to the defence had any reference to the sketch deleted and the defence was unaware that it existed until years later.

The High Court overturned Mallard's conviction and ordered a retrial. The Department of Public Prosecutions decided not to proceed with the charges against him. The Commission on Crime and Corruption investigated the Mallard case. It made 25 adverse findings against two senior police officers and 13 against the leading prosecutor. The Police Commissioner then stood down five police officers and apologised to Mallard.

In May 2009 Mallard was granted an extraordinarily generous $3.25 million by way of compensation for his wrongful conviction and the 12 years he spent in prison.

* *  * *

The scandals of WA Inc and the well-publicised miscarriages of justice were certainly at least partly responsible for the Government of Western Australia deciding to establish the Commission Against Crime and Corruption in 2003. That Commission was given three responsibilities: to help prevent misconduct by government agencies; to ensure that any allegations of misconduct are appropriately dealt with; and to assist the police fight organised crime. Any citizen may complain to the Commission, which has wide powers to compel people to answer questions. The investigations by the Commission have resulted in a considerable number of prosecutions. Those prosecutions have not always been successful and the Commission has – as a result – been widely criticised, but at least since its establishment it has given cause for anyone in Western Australia tempted to indulge in corruption to consider the consequences.

Chapter 23: *Land Rights*

When Australia was claimed as part of the British Empire, the country was considered by the British to be 'terra nullius' – land owned by no one. The administrators in each of the Australian colonies proceeded to grant settlers title to parcels of land with absolutely no regard for the aboriginals who were accustomed to living, hunting and gathering there.

The indigenous Australians had no way of proving to the satisfaction of the colonial authorities that they had any title to the land. British law required all transactions regarding real estate to be in writing. There was, however, one method of acquiring title to land informally and without documentary evidence that was recognised in British law – adverse possession. If an individual could prove to have enjoyed exclusive possession of land for 15 years, he or she could claim legal ownership. Aboriginal tribes had used areas of the land as hunting grounds for generations but the colonial authorities and the later state governments refused to recognise there was such a thing as native title.

The dispossession of the aboriginals in what are now the more densely populated areas of Australia was rapid and absolute. Disease and the Aboriginal Wars had reduced their numbers and forced them to retreat to the outback. When the question of native title eventually became a legal issue it was in those more remote parts of the country where indigenous Australians were still living in sufficient numbers to be able to exert political pressure.

The establishment of stations by pastoralists in the rangelands of Western Australia had serious consequences for the indigenous people living there. Cattle polluted waterholes and destroyed native vegetation. The pastoralists culled the kangaroos to reduce competition for the available feed, and by doing so made hunting difficult for the aboriginals. If any aboriginal person then killed cattle they were subjected to savage reprisals. Unable to live off the land, many aboriginals found employment as station hands or as domestic helpers. More often than not they were paid far less than a fair wage and treated badly.

In 1946 in the Pilbara some aboriginal stockmen, with the help of Don McLeod – an Australian Workers' Union delegate at Port Hedland – organised a strike for better pay and conditions. The authorities attempted to impose order and McLeod was arrested seven times, but the strike continued in some areas for about three years. A number of trade unions and the Women's Christian Temperance Union supported the strikers, and when the Seamen's Union placed a black ban on the shipment of wool from the Pilbara the State Government decided to intervene. McLeod claimed that a government representative promised that the strikers' demand would be met if they returned to work, but the government denied that any such promise had been made. Nevertheless, the strike did end and improved wages and conditions were negotiated for stockmen on a number of stations. Many stockmen refused to return to their subservient roles and some began to work cattle stations of their own as cooperatives or ventured into mining.

It was the 1966 strike at the Wave Hill Station in the Northern Territory that marked the beginning of the move for more than just reasonable conditions for aboriginal workers. There the Gurindji people led by Vincent Lingiari walked off work. They were offered an increase in pay, but they demanded the same pay as other employees received and then began to agitate for the return of the land to their tribe.

The campaign for land rights for Australia's indigenous population gathered momentum and gained the support of church groups and trade unionists. In 1967 the Federal Government held a referendum and the people of Australia overwhelmingly approved the amendment of Section 51 of the Commonwealth Constitution, allowing the Commonwealth Government power to make laws regarding aboriginal peoples. The Commonwealth then negotiated with the owners of Wave Hill Station and, as a result, part of the station was handed over to the Gurindji people.

About the same time, the people of the Yungngora tribe working on Noonkanbah Station near the Fitzroy River in Western Australia were demanding better pay and conditions. When their demands were rejected they walked off the station and became fringe dwellers at Fitzroy Crossing where they lived on social welfare payments.

In 1972 the state government decided to provide support by establishing the Aboriginal Land Trust. The Trust was commissioned to acquire land in order to hold and use it for the benefit of people of aboriginal descent. Members of the Yungngora tribe then asked the State Government to instruct the Trust to purchase Noonkanbah Station and allow them to run it. The Government obliged, and the Yungngora re-occupied Noonkanbah. When they discovered that the station was the subject of no less than 497 mining leases and an oil exploration permit, they took legal action to have the leases and the exploration permit cancelled. The magistrate who heard the case in Broome ruled that the mining rights had been lawfully acquired, and the law could not be negated by any moral or spiritual arguments.

Matters came to a head when two companies decided to drill near an aboriginal sacred site. The drillers arrived at the entrance to Noonkanbah with their drilling rig, but found the gate locked and protesters blocking access. The blockade attracted a great deal of publicity. Soon trade unionists, environmentalists and many other citizens voiced their support for the Noonkanbah people. The State Government eventually decided that it could not allow the aboriginals and other protesters to defy the law and, in 1980, sent a large detachment of police to clear the way for the drillers. The exploratory well discovered no oil or gas. The Yungngora people later succeeded in obtaining recognition of their claim to be the Traditional Owners of Noonkanbah Station.

There were three landmark court cases in the progress towards the recognition of the rights of aboriginals as Traditional Owners.

The first was Milirrpum v Nabalco Pty Ltd, heard by the Supreme Court of the Northern Territory in 1971. The Yolngu people sought an injunction to stop the establishment of a bauxite mine at the Gove Peninsular. The action failed and the judge ruled that the concept of native title was not recognised by the law of Australia.

The Whitlam Commonwealth Government then appointed Justice Edward Woodward, who had acted for Yolngu people in the case regarding the Gove Peninsular, to establish a Royal Commission to investigate how aboriginal land rights could be introduced. To avoid conflict with the various state governments, the Whitlam government commissioned Woodward to make findings only regarding land in the Northern Territory, which, at that stage, was under the control of the Commonwealth. The Fraser Liberal Government in 1976 followed up the findings of the Woodward Royal Commission by passing the Aboriginal Land Rights Act (Northern Territory) that allowed aboriginals to claim title over land if evidence of traditional association could be proved.

Not all state governments were prepared to follow the Commonwealth's lead. Land rights legislation was enacted in South Australia, New South Wales and Queensland but the Western Australian parliament has never passed a similar bill. In 1985 an attempt was made to give aboriginals in Western Australia a legislative basis for claiming land rights. A bill to enable that was passed by the Legislative Assembly, but was defeated in the Legislative Council.

More significant than Milirrpum v Nabalco were the Mabo cases.

Eddie Mabo and four other Meriam people set out to establish traditional title over the Murray Islands in the Torres Strait. The Queensland Government, in an attempt to retain control of the island, passed the Queensland Coast Islands Declamatory Act of 1985 that purported to abolish – retrospectively – any land title rights that may exist. The Meriam people approached the High Court to rule that the 1985 act could not be pleaded as a bar to their claim to title. The Court ruled that, if native title could be proved, the act would be a denial of the right to own and inherit property and so could not be pleaded. The action for native title by Mabo and others proceeded, and in 1992 the High Court in 1992 decided that Australia had never been terra nullius and that the Meriam people were entitled to possession, occupation, use and enjoyment of Murray Island.

The Western Australian Government responded to the Mabo judgement by passing the Land (Titles and Traditional Uses) Act of 1993 which was designed to keep Western Australian land firmly in the control of the Western Australian government. It proved to be yet another vain attempt to resist the gradual leaking of power from the state government to the Commonwealth.

Two groups of Australian aboriginals and the

Commonwealth Government commenced an action in the High Court to challenge the validity of the Western Australian statute.[60] The High Court decided that the statute was invalid, as it was contradiction of the findings in the Mabo case. Native title, the Court declared, was not completely extinguished when Britain claimed sovereignty over the whole state, as counsel for the Government of Western Australia had contended. Native title had just been extinguished, parcel by parcel, as land was granted as freehold to people and corporations, but it still existed in the rest of the state.

The Commonwealth Government subsequently passed the Native Title Act of 1993 that established a regime by which a claim to native title could be tested and, if proved, a determination made regarding who was entitled to claim it. The National Native Title Tribunal is now based in Perth and has registries in the other capital cities. It decides whether a claim meets the requirements of the Native Title Act, serves notice upon affected parties, and makes recommendations to the Federal Court which makes the final decisions. By July 2011 no less than 533 claims had been lodged with the Tribunal with respect to land in Western Australia.[61] Only 28 had been finalised. Well over half of the remaining claims were listed as undetermined. The rest have either been dismissed or withdrawn. Establishing native title to the satisfaction of the Tribunal has not proved to be easy.

The Commonwealth Native Title Act has had serious consequences for the Western Australian Government, individuals and corporations dealing with land in the state.

60 Western Australia v the Commonwealth (1995) 183 CLR 373
61 See the National Native Title Tribunal website at www.nntt.gov.au

Prior to the act, land in Western Australia had been either Crown Land – under the complete control of the state government – or private land owned by individuals or corporations with their entitlements secure and registered at the Land Titles Office. Now any Crown land – and that includes land held by government agencies, national parks and reserves, and pastoral leases – is liable to be affected by a claim of native title. The claim may be made by a category of individuals the exact membership of which may be a contentious issue. The rights conferred by the establishment of native title are derived from the traditional laws and customs of the claimants and therefore vary from case to case. Native title may be argued to co-exist with the rights of others regarding the land. No longer is there a clearly defined title to all the land in the state. The state government and corporations or individuals have to consult and negotiate with possible native title claimants when considering a development on Crown Land or pastoral leases. Even after an agreement has been reached, there is still the possibility of continuing dissent and protest.

A distinct thread in the history of Western Australia since federation has been the gradual taking of power from the state government by the Commonwealth. That is most evident in the matter of land rights, and the proposed gas hub near Broome well illustrates this. No matter what the Kimberley Land Council and the state government decide, in the end the final decision as to whether the gas hub is to be built – and if so just where – will be made by the Federal Minister for the Environment.

The powers of the Commonwealth Government are defined in Section 51 of the Constitution and there is no mention of the environment in that section, but the Commonwealth has a way of assuming additional powers. It can claim it is discharging obligations it has under international agreements entered into in exercise of its 'external affairs' powers. It is a party to a number of international agreements designed to protect the environment. The Commonwealth's *Environment Protection and Biodiversity Protection Act 1999* would justify any claim the Minister might make that he is entitled to interfere in the development at Tom Price Point.

It is heartening to be able to conclude this concise history of Western Australia by reporting what could be a turning point in the history of the indigenous Australians.

The enormous wealth being derived from the iron ore and the oil and gas in the Pilbara has so far brought little or no benefit to the indigenous people of the area – to the contrary, it has been estimated that more aboriginal men in the Pilbara are in prison than in employment.

In late 2011 Rio Tinto announced that over a period of about seven years it has been negotiating with the five aboriginal groups who might be entitled to establish a claim to native title over about 70,000 square kilometres of the Pilbara. An agreement had been reached under the terms of which the company will pay $2 billion to the five groups over 40 years, train and employ aboriginal workers, support aboriginal businesses and protect any sites of significance. In return, the company has the approval of all potential Traditional Owners for the establishment of something like 30 new mines in the Pilbara with the potential to increase its sales of iron ore to 400 million tonnes per annum. If that agreement enables a considerable number of those five groups to free themselves from reliance upon welfare handouts and enjoy the dignity of being respected members of the State's workforce and the benefits of having a reasonable income, native title must be regarded as a win for all Australians.

Bibliography

Barry, Paul. *The Rise and Fall of Allan Bond.* Bantam Books, 1990

Benedictine Community. *The Story of New Norcia.* The Benedictine Community of New Norcia, 1970

Burvill. George H. *Agriculture in Western Australia 1829-1979.* University of Western Australia Press, 1979

'Cygnet'. *Swan River Booklets No. 4.* Paterson and Brokensha Pty Ltd. Perth, 1935

Dowson. John. *Old Albany.* Albany Chamber of Commerce and Industry, 2008

Evans. A.G. *C.J.O'Connor, His Life and Legacy.* University of Western Australia Press, 2001

Eyre. Edward John. *Journals of Expedition and Discovery and Overland from Adelaide to King George Sound in the Years 1840-1841.* T & W Boone, 1845

Fitzsimons. Peter. *Charles Kingsford Smith and Those Magnificent Men.* Harper Collins, 2009

Flannery, Tim. *The Explorers.* The Text Publishing Company, 1998

Hasluck, Alexandra. *Thomas Peel of Swan River.* Melbourne University Press, 1965

Hasluck, Alexandra. *Portrait with Backgound – the Life of Georgiana Molloy.* Oxford University Press, 1955

Heeres, J.E. (ed.) *Abel Jannsxoon's Journal of discovery of Van Dieman's Land and New Zealand.* N.A.Kovach, Los Angeles, 1965

Heeres. J.E. *The Part Borne by the Dutch in the Discovery of Australia 1606-1765.* Luzac & Co, London, 1899

Masefield, John. *Dampier's Voyages.* E. Grant Richards, London, 1906

Nairn, John *Western Australia's Tempestuous History.* North Stirling Press, Perth, 1977

Ogle, Nathaniel. *The Colony of Western Australia: A Manual for Emigrants.* James Fraser, London, 1839. Reprinted by James Ferguson, Sydney, in association with the Royal Australian Historical Society

Robin, A de Q. *Matthew Blagden Hale – The Life of an Australian Pioneer Bishop.* Melbourne Hawthorn Press, 1976

Shann E.O.G. *Cattle Chosen.* The University of Western Australia Press, 1926

Stannage C.T. (ed.) *Convictism in Western Australia.* University of Western Australia, 1981

Battye J.S. *Western Australia – A History from its Discovery to the Inauguration of the Commonwealth.* Oxford University Press, 1924

W.A. Historical Society. *Early Days – Journals and Proceedings.* Reproduced from the original printings for the Royal Historical Society in 1977 by West Australian Newspapers Ltd

Wollaston J. R. *Wollaston's Picton Journals.* C.H.Pitman and Sons, 1948

Index

ALSO AVAILABLE FROM RUSSELL EARLS DAVIS

Bligh in Australia
A new appraisal of William Bligh and the Rum Rebellion

The Rum Rebellion has, for generations, been told to school children as one of the better stories of Australian History - how Bligh, the villain of Hollywood's version of the Bounty mutiny story, was a tyrant deposed by the New South Wales Corps and dragged out from his hiding place under a bed.

It has even been said – and this is just as far from the truth - that the overthrowing of Governor Bligh was a victory for democracy and colonial self- government.

Although there have been two excellent, scholarly works that have told the truth about the Rum Rebellion, one focuses very much on the overall story of the time, while the other focuses on the legal situation prevailing. Neither combines the historical with the legal situation and presents a good story in which a number of interesting characters played a significant role.

Russell Earls Davis presents an account that, as far as possible from the available evidence, tells us what actually did happen in the lead up to the Rum Rebellion and of the legal and political aspects of the aftermath.

Bligh in Australia lends impetus to the growing recent trend to recognise that William Bligh was no tyrant or coward, as his mutinous enemies alleged, but an incredibly strong-willed servant of the British Government who did precisely – perhaps sometimes too precisely – what he had been ordered. On the Bounty, and again in New South Wales, he faced situations where the forces against him would have utterly defeated many a lesser man, yet in the end he prevailed.

Paperback $24.95   ISBN: 9781921683503

ALSO AVAILABLE FROM WOODSLANE

Arthur Phillip
Australia's First Governor

By Derek Parker

Over the two centuries since his appointment, commentators have been as surprised at the choice of Arthur Phillip as Governor of the new penal colony at New South Wales as some were at the time (the First Lord of the Admiralty, to mention only the most distinguished critic). But was it really so surprising? What did the Home Office and the Admiralty expect of a man who was to navigate a fleet to the antipodes, and when he got it there unload its cargo of unregenerate criminals and forge them into some sort of a working colony? Apart from the necessary seamanship, they needed a man with a cool head who understood men and how to control them, a man capable of governing himself, possessed of calm and understanding and a thorough grasp of reality, with complete loyalty to the Crown and Government and a determination to plan and carry through an enterprise unlike any other within living memory. Fortunately, there were one or two men at the Admiralty who understood that Arthur Phillip possessed all these credentials. This new biography covers Phillip's whole life, but has a particular focus on his selection for the role of Governor, the preparation of the first fleet, the journey from England, the establishment of the Colony and Phillip's governorship.

Hardback $44.95 ISBN: 9781921203992
Paperback $24.95 ISBN: 9781921683480

ALSO AVAILABLE FROM WOODSLANE

Governor Macquarie
His life, times and revolutionary vision for Australia

By Derek Parker

The first new biography of Lachlan Macquarie in decades, this book draws on a wealth of sources, both in Australia and overseas, to paint a picture of the man and his times. It must be seen as one of the great ironies of Australian history that, as far as the British Government was concerned, he failed in his duty as Governor of New South Wales – as was clearly documented to official minds in the official report compiled by Commissioner John Bigge. This report concluded that while Governor Macquarie had certainly supervised the building in New South Wales of some good roads and some handsome buildings (if at far too high a cost to the British taxpayers), under his government the Colony had ceased to be what it was required to be: a place with a reputation for cruelty and hopelessness so terrifying that the very threat of being banished there would strike terror into the heart of any prospective malefactor. Macquarie had in fact a vision shared by few others that New South Wales – indeed the whole of New Holland – had the potential to become 'one of the greatest and most flourishing colonies belonging to the British Empire', and became determined to do his part in steering the fledgling community in that direction.

Paperback $24.95 ISBN: 9781921606915

ALSO AVAILABLE FROM WOODSLANE

Outback
The Discovery of Australia's Interior

By Derek Parker

In 1800, while the coast of Australia had finally been charted, the vast interior of the continent, and routes across its deserts and mountains from north to south and east to west lay all undiscovered. By 1874, its lands had been all but won. Derek Parker's exciting book gathers together the stories of those intrepid explorers who, often against great odds, on journeys of months or even years, beat starvation, inadequate information and mapping, disease and loss, to forge a routes which would enable the country's development. From early explorers, who were generally escaped convicts, to the son of a Lincolnshire surgeon who coined the name 'Australia'; from explorers Major Mitchell, who slaughtered aborigines, to Sir George Grey, who learnt their language, recorded their culture and came to love and understand them; and from the greatest overland expedition in Australian history in 1844 to continued failed attempts to find a mythical 'inland sea', this is a fascinating read.

Paperback $24.95 ISBN: 9781921203923

ALSO AVAILABLE FROM WOODSLANE

Banjo Paterson
The Man who wrote Waltzing Matilda

By Derek Parker

A.B. 'Banjo' Paterson was not simply the author of the words of 'Waltzing Matilda', Australia's unofficial national anthem, and many other classic ballads such as 'The Man from Snowy River' and 'Clancy of the Overflow'. Though it is now almost forgotten, he was a first-rate war correspondent for the Sydney Morning Herald and his dispatches from the Boer War are as vivid and exciting to read today as when they were frantically scribbled under the guns of Boer sharp-shooters. He was a friend of 'Breaker' Morant, whose notorious trial and execution was one of the sensations of that war. He was also an expert horseman, a man who knew everything there was to be known about horses and horse-racing, winning prizes at polo matches and race meetings. Returning from South Africa, The Banjo (as he always signed himself) worked for Sydney newspapers, and travelled to China and England (where he stayed with his friend, the poet Rudyard Kipling), and for a while led a relatively sedentary life as editor of The Sydney Evening News. At the outbreak of World War One, he served as an ambulance driver in France, and finally to Egypt where he headed a team of rough-riders and trained horses. Major Paterson then edited The Sportsman in Sydney and became a popular and well-known broadcaster in the early days of radio. Ironically, by the time he died everyone Aussie knew 'Waltzing Matilda' but scarcely anyone could have told you they had been written by 'Banjo' – he'd sold the copyright years before for £5!

Hardback $34.95   ISBN: 9781921606076
Paperback $24.95   ISBN: 9781921683480

ALSO AVAILABLE FROM WOODSLANE

This Accursed Land
Douglas Mawson's incredible Antarctic journey

By Lennard Bickel

Antarctica is not generally friendly to life, and is aggressively hostile to human life, and yet for the last 150 years explorers have pitted themselves against it time and again. Frequently, and particularly during the 'heroic' age of the first couple of decades of the twentieth century, their efforts were met with extreme danger and even death. The names Scott, Shackleton and Amundsen are writ especially large in our cultural history because of their harrowing journeys to the ice continent. Australian Douglas Mawson's name does not shine quite as brightly, which ironically gives him much credit: he was not so much a 'pole-chaser' as a committed scientist, and won more secrets from Antarctica than his more famous contemporaries put together; and careful planning meant that he usually suffered less from the mishaps that plagued others. And yet, just once, catastrophe did strike. Three hundred miles from base-camp – three hundred miles of the coldest, most lethal territory on earth – Mawson lost one of his two companions and most of his supplies down a crevasse. Soon after the survivors' attempt to claw back to base began, his other companion died of the horrendous conditions they had to bear. This disaster, and Mawson's incredible 6-week solo journey back to base – described by Sir Edmund Hilary as the greatest story of lone survival in polar exploration – make up the thrilling narrative of Lennard Bickel's classic book.

Paperback $29.95 ISBN: 9781921683046